THE LEADE____ ____ __ __ TO
ORGANIZATIONA_ ON

CHANGE
YOUR
CULTURE
CHANGE
EVERYTHING

SAM CHAND

Change Your Culture, Change Everything: The Leader's Guide to Transforming Organizational Culture

by Sam Chand
copyright ©2017

Trade paperback ISBN: 978-1-943294-59-6

Cover design by Vanessa Mendozzi

CONTENTS

CHAPTER 1

CULTURE TRUMPS VISION

Unless commitment is made, there are only promises and hopes . . . but no plans. —PETER DRUCKER

A CHURCH IN THE MIDWEST GREW rapidly, but the growth curve gradually flattened. In recent years, they saw almost no growth at all. In the early days of explosive growth, the senior pastor taught seminars and spoke at national conferences to instruct other pastors in how to grow their churches, but in the past few years, he received very few invitations to speak. When the curve began to flatten, he took his senior staff to hear noted speakers. Surely, he thought, they could learn something new and overcome stagnation. When that didn't fix things, they hired consultants to analyze the situation and prescribe a solution. When this strategy didn't effect the change they wanted, the senior pastor began "cleaning house." He hired and fired so many people that the offices needed revolving doors. Still, the church didn't grow.

Out of frustration, the pastor left the church. He moved his family a few miles away and started another church with about two hundred people who followed him there. Some would call this a church plant; I think it was a glorified church split.

At the original church, a new pastor came into the office full of fresh ideas and a clear vision of where the church could go; that's exactly why he was selected. After a long, grueling first eighteen months with the new pastor on the job, however, the church's growth curve had barely budged. When he called me, he was frustrated and tired. In our first meeting, he told me sadly, "I don't understand. We spent time and money to re-energize the congregation. We took our top staff on a retreat to instill the new vision into them. We hired more staff, and we reformatted our worship experience. We started plenty of new programs. We redesigned our stage set. We created a killer Web site, reconfigured our offices, redecorated to create a fresh ambiance, and designed a new logo for the church. We even wrote a song about how great we are! But none of this has made a bit of difference. We haven't gone backward, and I'm glad of that, but I thought we'd be way ahead of where we are today." He paused for a second and then asked, "What am I missing?"

This senior pastor had done a lot of good things, but he failed to understand the impact of the existing organizational culture on his new, exciting vision for the church. It was like changing the engine on a sports car to make it faster, but it was spinning its wheels in the mud.

Culture—not vision or strategy—is the most powerful factor in any organization. It determines the receptivity of staff and volunteers to new ideas, unleashes or dampens creativity, builds or erodes enthusiasm, and creates a sense of pride or deep discouragement about working or being involved there. Ultimately, the culture of an organization—particularly in churches and nonprofit organizations, but also in any organization—shapes individual morale, teamwork, effectiveness, and outcomes. In an article in the magazine *Executive Leadership*, Dick Clark explains how he took the pharmaceutical firm Merck to a higher level: "The fact is, culture eats strategy for lunch. You can have a good strategy in place, but if you don't have the culture and the enabling systems, the [negative] culture of the organization will defeat the strategy."[1] To help you uncover the nature of your existing culture and identify the steps of change, this book examines the full range of cultural health, from inspiring to toxic, and describes the seven keys of CULTURE:

1. Control
2. Understanding
3. Leadership
4. Trust
5. Unafraid
6. Responsive
7. Execution

Insight is the first—and crucial—step toward change.

LOOKING AT THE LANDSCAPE

In the past decade or so, dozens of books and countless articles have been written about the importance of corporate culture, but relatively few churches and nonprofit organizations have taken the arduous (but necessary) steps to assess, correct, and change their culture. First, we need to understand what we mean by the term *organizational culture*. It is the personality of the church or nonprofit.

Organizational culture includes tangibles and intangibles. The things we can see are the way people dress and behave, the look of the corporate offices, and the messages of posters on the walls. The intangibles may be harder to grasp, but they give a better read on the organization's true personality. The organization's values (stated and unstated), beliefs, and assumptions; what and how success is celebrated; how problems are addressed; the manifestations of trust and respect at all levels of the organization—these are the intangible elements of culture. Every group in society—family, town, state, nation, company, church, civic group, team, and any other gathering of people—has a culture, sometimes clearly identified but often camouflaged.

Many leaders confuse culture with vision and strategy, but they are very different. Vision and strategy usually focus on products, services, and outcomes, but culture is about the people—the most valuable asset in the organization. The way people are treated, the way they treat their peers, and their response to their leaders is the air people breathe. If that air is clean and healthy, people thrive and the organization succeeds, but to the extent that it is toxic, energy subsides, creativity lags, conflicts multiply, and production declines.

The inputs into the "cultural system" include the stories that surround the staff's experiences; shared goals and responsibilities; respect and care for people; balance between bold leadership and listening; and clear, regular communication. The outcomes include the reputation of the leader, the reputation of the organization, the attractiveness of the church or nonprofit to prospective new staff members, a measure of pride in being a part of the organization, and a positive impact on the entire community.

To see a few snapshots of a church's culture, we might ask these questions:

• Who are the heroes? What makes them heroes? Who determines who the heroes are?

• When someone inquires, "Tell me about your church or nonprofit," what stories are told?

- How much does the average staff member feel he or she has input into the direction and strategy of the church or nonprofit?

- Who has the ear of the top leaders? How did these people win a hearing with the leaders?

- What are the meaningful rituals? What message do they convey to those in the organization and those outside it?

- Who is rewarded, and for what accomplishments?

- What is the level of loyalty up and down the organizational chart? What factors build loyalty?

- What is the level of creativity and enthusiasm throughout the organization?

- When an objective observer spends an hour watching people interact in the offices, what mood does he or she pick up?

- How are decisions made, deferred, or delayed?

- Who are the nonpositional power brokers, the people who have authority based on the respect they've earned but who don't have authoritative titles?

- Where are control problems and power struggles most evident?

- How is "turf" defined and protected?

The shape of an organization's culture begins at the top level. The leader's integrity, competence, and care for staff members create the environment where people excel . . . or not. In his book *The Five Dysfunctions of a Team,* Patrick Lencioni observes that trust is the most powerful trait in shaping a positive culture, and trust thrives on honesty. He writes, "When there is an absence of trust, it stems from a leader's unwillingness to be vulnerable with the group," and "leaders who are not genuinely open with one another about their mistakes and weaknesses make it impossible to build a foundation of trust."[2]

A healthy culture inspires and stimulates all staff members—whether they're in the boardroom or the mailroom—to give their best because they are convinced their ideas will be valued. In a creative, supportive environment, people are less threatened by their own mistakes and by others' failures. Problems are viewed through a different lens: they become opportunities for growth, not causes for condemnation. Certainly, there has to be a balance between meeting immediate organizational goals and patient listening, but the vast majority of staff members are thrilled when anyone, especially the top exec, cares enough to listen at all. Employees who feel valued work harder, are more productive, and add value to the organization's purpose. A healthy culture works for everybody.

KEY PRINCIPLES

As we begin our examination of organizational culture, I want to communicate some important principles.

CULTURE IS THE MOST POWERFUL FACTOR IN ANY ORGANIZATION

I travel quite a bit, and I've become a student of hotels around the world. In some cases, I've noticed a significant difference between hotels, even when the rooms actually cost about the same. The difference is in the quality of service. I've stayed in some very nice hotels where it seemed that my coming was a nuisance to the staff. No one opened the door for me or offered to lug my suitcase and boxes into the lobby.

But I've also enjoyed very different experiences at some hotels. Not long ago, I stayed at a Ritz Carlton. When the car dropped me off, a man opened my door and greeted me by saying, "Welcome to the Ritz Carlton, Dr. Chand." I wondered, *Did I leave a nametag on?* No, but somehow he knew I was coming and went out of his way to greet me. The woman at the desk also knew my name (How did they do that?), and she gave me a key without hesitation. At the Ritz Carlton, though, every staff member has authority to do whatever it takes to care for a guest.

The slogan for the Ritz Carlton Hotels is "Ladies and gentlemen serving ladies and gentlemen." Can you see how this simple but profound statement reflects their inherent corporate culture? By treating each employee with dignity, the company fills his or her need for significance, and warmhearted service flows out of each one like a flood.

I can imagine that the other hotel chains had some kind of written statement to inform employees that they need to serve their guests, but its statement didn't create a culture of service like the one at the Ritz. In fact, it didn't seem to make even a dent. Vision statements, strategies, and goals are very good tools, but they can't compare in importance to the culture. The culture of an organization is the platform for building a strong church or nonprofit. It is the fertile soil for growing creativity and passion for excellence, and the rocket fuel for reaching new heights in excellence and accomplishments.

CULTURE IS USUALLY UNNOTICED, UNSPOKEN, AND UNEXAMINED

How often do we think about the air we breathe? It's so pervasive that we don't even give it a thought. It's absolutely essential for life, but only a few climatologists spend time analyzing it. Organizational culture is like the air; it's all around us, shaping every moment of every day, but we seldom notice it at all.

Most leaders of churches and nonprofit organizations focus almost all their energies on the tangibles of growth and donations. Their means to fulfill their goals are a clear, compelling vision and a workable strategy. Those are important components, but they only succeed if the underlying culture stimulates creativity, passion, and productivity throughout the organization. Top leaders need to spend at least as much time analyzing their culture as they do crafting their new vision, strategy, and marketing plans.

Toxic culture is like carbon monoxide: you don't see or smell it, but you wake up dead!

CULTURE DETERMINES HOW PEOPLE RESPOND TO VISION AND LEADERSHIP

For one reason or another, some top leaders have an innate distrust of their staff. Their mode of leadership, then, is to tightly control everything their people do. They may smile while they're squeezing employees, but their people don't feel valued when they experience close scrutiny and micromanagement. On the other end of the continuum, a few leaders take a handsoff approach. They think their role is to push the ball and just let it roll wherever it goes. They don't give their staff members direction or feedback, so their people wander around confused and frustrated. And some leaders rule by ambivalence and ambiguity. They use the unknown to provoke anxiety and keep people off balance, and then they wonder why people are tentative, indecisive, and nonproductive. In these toxic cultures, people resent leaders instead of respecting them, their level of motivation wanes, they complain a lot to anyone who will listen (and some who don't want to), and they aren't very productive.

The intangibles of respect and trust transform a church culture into a beehive of thinking, creating, and working together to accomplish grand goals. When staff members feel valued, they far more readily embrace a leader's vision. Even if they disagree or don't understand, they are more willing to give the benefit of the doubt and pitch in.

Whenever I uncover the culture of an organization, I instinctively ask two questions: *Would I want someone in my family to work here?* and *Would I want to work here?*

CULTURE MOST OFTEN SURFACES AND IS ADDRESSED IN NEGATIVE EXPERIENCES

All of us would like to believe that we are incredibly perceptive and responsive, but the truth is that most of us stay stuck in the same ruts in our lives until something shakes us out of them. These pervasive patterns of behavior are too big for quick fixes. They force us to take a long, hard look at our organizations and ourselves. Only with deep reflection, accurate information, and courage can we take the necessary steps of change.

Make no mistake: most competent leaders rose to their positions because they are supremely confident in their abilities. They're convinced they know how to run the organization, and they've fixed enough problems to fill volumes of books. But sooner or later, they may run into difficulties that defy their attempts to fix them. Power struggles consume their top levels of leadership, complaints from staff members and church members sour the air each day, and their new vision for growth isn't getting any traction at all among volunteers and the people in the pews. When the difficulty revolves around people, it's probably a culture problem that won't be solved by any vision or strategy. The only solution is to change the culture.

Culture problems, by their nature, are never solved quickly. They require a clear understanding of the problem, a commitment to systemic change, and patience and persistence to see change take root.

Far too often, we try to minimize difficulties and act as if they didn't matter, we excuse ourselves and say it's not our fault, or we point the accusatory finger at others. None of these responses leads to wisdom and change. A far more healthy and productive reaction is to stop, notice what happened, and ask, "Is there something more than meets the eye going on here?" That's how we uncover a flawed culture so that we can address it.

CULTURE IS HARD TO CHANGE, BUT CHANGE RESULTS IN MULTI-PLIED BENEFIT

I don't want to minimize the mountain I'm asking leaders to climb. It's a steep and difficult journey, but those who have successfully negotiated it have never regretted a moment on the path. When they see staff members with a compelling sense of purpose, when they hear exciting stories that become part of the organization's history, when they see tears in people's eyes because they believe so much in what they're doing, and when they see them respond with joy and enthusiasm to make a good strategy even better, they know it's been worth it. If you're a senior pastor, value the input of men and women who love you enough to tell you the truth. Talk to people far removed from the seat of power; ask them honest questions about what they see, think, and feel about the organization.

So, have you been investing your time and energies into crafting and articulating your organization's vision, only to find that people aren't as receptive as you hoped? When there's a disconnect between a leader's vision and the receptivity of the staff, the problem isn't with the vision; it's the culture. Most leaders don't invest much in their church's culture simply because they assume it's "just fine." I believe, though, that great leaders devote as many resources to building and shaping their organization's culture as they invest in vision and strategy. In fact, vision and strategy simply can't succeed without a positive, healthy culture.

THIS BOOK IS FOR YOU IF . . .

As I've talked about these principles to leaders around the world, some have asked if ministry or department heads can implement the changes in this book even if their supervisors don't ever change. Yes, they can courageously take steps to change the culture in their worlds, but they'll always be fighting against the negative pressures from the executive suite. I've known many church ministry leaders and department heads who "protected" their people from the abuses of their bosses, but they often paid a high price. In most cases, they were glad to do that because they really cared for their people, but eventually, many of these dear, brave men and women were forced out, or they left simply because they couldn't take it anymore.

MY PROMISE TO YOU

If you'll read and reflect honestly on the principles in this book, I believe that you'll have a new appreciation for the impact of your organizational culture on every aspect of life. These insights will enable you to make a strong connection between culture and vision so that you always communicate vision *in light of* your culture. A positive culture will act as an accelerant for your vision. With a new appreciation for your culture, you'll empower your staff members to do their very best—and love doing it. You will create the context for vision to grow. When your people feel valued, their enthusiasm will electrify your church! To make all this happen, this book outlines a process to implement the changes necessary for you, your top leadership team, and all the rest of your leaders.

The principles and practices in this book are designed to equip you to be the leader you've always wanted to be. There's no magic formula—quite the contrary. Changing your organization's culture will be one of the most challenging processes you've ever implemented, but I guarantee you, you'll be glad you did.

• • •

As you get started, I recommend you visit *FreeCultureSurvey. com* and take the survey developed by Mr. Pat Springle, Professor Tom Snider and myself. This survey was designed to help leaders obtain an accurate assessment of the culture of their teams.

CHAPTER 2
CULTURE KILLERS

Few things help an individual more than to place responsibility upon him, and to let him know that you trust him. —BOOKER T. WASHINGTON

ON A FEW OCCASIONS WHEN I walk into the offices of an organization where I've been asked to consult with the leadership team, I sense immediately that something's wrong. At that moment, it's too early to put my finger on the problem, but after meeting just a few people, I can sense a pervasive anxiety or confusion. If just one person is uncomfortable, I conclude that he or she is having a bad day. If, however, I pick up negative vibes from several people, I wonder if the culture has a systemic problem. The question I always ask myself when I sense a troubled culture is, *Why hasn't someone done something about it already? Don't they see it, too?* The answer is no. The dysfunction in the culture has become entirely normal. It's the way things have been and the way, people assume, they will always be.

Of course, cultures can change, but only when top leaders have the courage to take an objective appraisal of reality. When they don't recognize culture killers, toxic agents continue to infect every corner of the church or nonprofit organization. The first step, then, is to uncover and face the truth.

Churches and nonprofits have a wide range of personalities. They may produce very different services, but a few common traits characterize healthy organizations, and a set of opposite traits characterizes those that aren't healthy. For our purposes, I want to plot the range of cultures on a five-point continuum:

<—INSPIRING—ACCEPTING—STAGNANT—DISCOURAGING—TOXIC—>

We'll use the metaphor of a race car to illustrate the differences. Think of a high-performance Indy car, finely tuned and built for speed. The car represents the organization's vision and strategy. The car, though, can go only as fast as the road allows, and the culture is the road. Are you ready? Let's take a ride.

INSPIRING CULTURES

Indy cars fly along the ground at amazing speeds on smooth, dry racetracks. That's the image of inspiring cultures. The spirit of the organization encourages people to bring their best to work each day, and together, they accomplish amazing things.

CHARACTERISTICS OF INSPIRING CULTURES

- The leaders of these organizations give clear direction, but they aren't authoritarian; they value the input of every person. Authority is decentralized.
- Leaders cultivate an atmosphere of trust and respect.

- People throughout the organization believe that what they do each day really matters—to themselves, to their teams, to the church or nonprofit, and to their constituents.

- These organizations have high but realistic expectations. They set high goals, train people, give them the resources they need, stay connected throughout the process, and encourage them to succeed.

- Creativity is rewarded, and failures are viewed as steppingstones of growth. In fact, failure is seen as an essential part of the process of innovation, not a fatal flaw.

- There are few if any turf battles, so communication flows up and down the organizational chart and between departments.

- Top leaders retrain or replace ministry leaders who can't provide a positive work environment for their teams.

- There is a powerful synergy between relationships and organizational goals.

- The organization invests significantly and systematically in creating and building a healthy culture.

- Leaders regularly celebrate success throughout the organization, and they even celebrate those who leave and find success elsewhere.

- These organizations are a magnet for job applicants. They have their pick of the best and brightest.

ACCEPTING CULTURES

The road for some churches and nonprofit organizations is fairly smooth, but a little bumpy with a few potholes here and there. On this track, the Indy car has to slow down a bit to be sure to miss the holes and navigate the rough spots. Still, the race car makes great progress. Accepting cultures are very good places to work, for staff, volunteers, and people in the community.

CHARACTERISTICS OF ACCEPTING CULTURES

- The overall atmosphere is very positive, but there are a few topics that are taboo, or there are a few incompetent leaders who remain in the job too long. These unresolved issues and problematic leaders are the bumps and potholes that create tension.

- Generally, most people in the organization are supportive of each other's roles and goals. Communication is a strength, and people don't feel the need to defend their turf.

- Some difficult decisions are avoided instead of addressed expeditiously. For instance, leaving a poor ministry leader in place too long erodes the trust and drive of those who serve in that office.

- Most people who work in these churches and nonprofits think they are the best ones they've ever experienced. They love the blend of clear goals and strong relationships, and they are highly motivated to do their best.

- The senior leaders in these organizations invest in developing people and the culture. If they were more assertive about taking care of problems in the culture, they could be even more successful.

- These organizations enjoy a strong reputation, so they attract a lot of applicants. However, the new hires who are placed under incompetent ministry leaders are deeply disappointed.

STAGNANT CULTURES

Many organizations begin with a clear vision and great teamwork, but find that sooner or later, their culture loses energy and stagnates. The vision may still be as clear as it has ever been, but the atmosphere is like a humid summer day in Houston—so oppressive it makes you wilt! In these organizations, the Indy car finds itself on a dirt road full of ruts and holes, a road more suited to a pickup than a race car. To make much progress at all, the car moves slowly to avoid damage. At the end of each day, the driver is worn out but hasn't gone very far.

CHARACTERISTICS OF STAGNANT CULTURES

- The leadership team sees staff members as production units, not people. The staff members are valuable when—and only when—they produce. All praise is based on performance, very little if any on character.

- Staff members tolerate their leaders, but they don't trust or respect them. They still do their work, but only the most ambitious invest themselves in the success of the organization.

- The only heroes are the top executives, and the employees suspect that these top leaders are making a bundle, or at least receiving lots of accolades, at their expense. They resent it, too.

- Without trust, respect, and loyalty, people feel compelled to defend their turf, hang on to power, and limit communication. In this atmosphere, relatively small problems quickly escalate.

- Complaining becomes the staff members' pastime. Things aren't quite bad enough to prompt open rebellion, but a few disgruntled people are thinking about it!

- The leadership team isn't happy with the lack of enthusiasm and declining productivity, so they treat staff as if they were wayward teenagers. They try anything to control them: anger, pleading, threats, rewards, ignoring them, micromanaging them . . . but nothing works.

With only a few exceptions, people become clock-watchers and check-cashers, caring little for the leader's vision. The whole organization lives in a status quo of lethargy.

To correct the problem, the leaders may send people to seminars or hire consultants, but the top people aren't willing to take responsibility and make significant changes. It's always somebody else's fault.

These organizations usually attract people with low expectations and low motivation, but they may attract a few who believe their personal mission is to bring life to the organization. These individuals usually give up after a few months.

DISCOURAGING CULTURES

A few organizations suck the life out of their employees, leaving them hurt, angry, and confused. Every church and nonprofit encounters problems, but good ones make a point of resolving difficulties so that they can rebuild trust and achieve their goals. Discouraging cultures, though, live with the ghosts of countless unresolved problems and unhealed wounds. These organizations may still have clear, bold visions and effective strategies, but their people spend most of their time protecting themselves instead of devoting their energies to the success of the organization. The church's vision and strategy are like an Indy car stuck in the mud. The energy of the engine is wasted in spinning tires.

CHARACTERISTICS OF DISCOURAGING CULTURES

It's all about the top people: their prestige and their power. They act as though everybody else in the organization exists only to make them more successful, and most of the staff members deeply resent it.

People spend as much time trying to survive the power struggles, protecting themselves from more hurt, and analyzing the top people's pathology as they spend doing the work of the ministry. Staff may become fiercely loyal to a supervisor who protects them, but they actively seek to undermine any perceived adversary.

As the benchmarks of success decline, the top leaders become more authoritarian and threatening. They demand compliance and loyalty, and they defy anyone who disagrees with them or even offers another opinion. One man who worked in a nationally known church told me, "The ministry director told me that I had to work eighty hours a week or I could leave. I'm a salaried employee, so I don't get overtime. Basically, he was saying, 'We don't care about you at all. We *own* you.' That day, I started looking for another job."

The leadership team often tries to remedy the problems, but with the wrong analysis and the wrong solutions. They seldom look in the mirror to find a culprit. Instead, the blame is always put on "incompetent" or "unmotivated" people throughout the organization, but these are the only ones who are willing to stay employed there!

When these leaders communicate a new vision, nobody cares. They've heard it before, and they don't trust that anything will be different this time.

These organizations attract malcontents, sycophants, and desperate people who can't find a job anywhere else.

TOXIC CULTURES

Strangely, some of the most toxic organizations have the most charming leaders. To people on the outside looking in, these senior leaders and nonprofit executives present themselves as gracious, gifted leaders, but those who see them every day are the victims of their fangs and venom! In these cultures, the Indy car is on the road, but the bridge is out! Disaster is waiting for those who stay on board.

CHARACTERISTICS OF TOXIC CULTURES

- Leaders create a "closed system," so any advice and creative ideas from the outside are suspect from the start. In his insightful book *Incest in the Organizational Family*, William White observes that these systems breed bad ideas, bad behaviors, and bad values into the organization over and over again. That's why he calls it incest.

- Individual rights and the dignity of staff members are surrendered to the powerful elite. People are expected to do as they are told—nothing less and nothing else. The organization's leaders believe they "own" every employee. They have exceptionally high expectations of workers, but they offer them little or no autonomy to make decisions.

- Fear becomes the dominating motivational factor of the organization, and those who choose to stay meekly comply—most of the time. Many, though, are too afraid to leave. They've noticed that when people even think about leaving, they're severely criticized for being "disloyal."

- Turf battles are the accepted sport of the organization, and open warfare becomes normal. Suspicion and resentment poison lines of communication, so even the simplest directive becomes a weapon.

- Leaders delegate responsibility but fail to give authority to people to fulfill their roles.

- Creativity and risk-taking have long vanished, and in fact, these traits threaten the status of the bosses as the only ones who know anything. In this environment, pathology is rewarded and health is punished.

- Ethical, financial, or sexual lapses may occur, but staff members are expected to turn a blind eye. The leaders may constantly look over their shoulders to see if they've been caught.

- These organizations run off good people, and they attract only the naïve or truly desperate.

In my experience, the spectrum of cultures I've described falls along a bell curve. I've found relatively few truly inspiring organizations, but thankfully, I haven't encountered many that are genuinely toxic. Most churches and nonprofits fall in the middle three categories. Looking at the top end of the scale, we shouldn't assume that inspiring and accepting organizations simply don't have problems and that this is why they excel. Quite the contrary. They all experience difficulties, but the leaders of healthy organizations are steadfastly committed to resolving problems, not with a heavy hand to rigidly control people, but by treating everyone with respect. They work hard to continue to build their cultures, taking nothing for granted. An incestuous organization continually breeds bad genes back into the system, but healthy companies invite new ideas and creative input from every imaginable source. A significant element of their stimulating environment is their thirst for growth and development.

POTHOLES, MUD, PITS, AND COLLAPSED BRIDGES

The most powerful features of an organizational culture are trust and respect. With them, almost any problem can be resolved, or at least people learn valuable lessons from difficult experiences, and in the process even learn to trust each other more. But without trust and respect, even the smallest molehill soon morphs into an Everest. The most common hazards we face are

- Unrealistic demands
- Blaming others
- Feeling threatened by others' success
- Power struggles

- Dishonesty
- Creating an atmosphere of fear
- Using people instead of valuing them
- Unclear vision, strategy, goals, and values
- A lack of authenticity

Let's look at some of the potholes, mud pits, and collapsed bridges that threaten to slow, stall, or crash our Indy car.

UNREALISTIC DEMANDS

There's nothing in the world wrong with having high expectations of staff members, so long as there is always a healthy dose of realism in an atmosphere that welcomes give-and-take, creativity, and problem solving at all levels. When times are tough, the easiest thing for them to do is pressure their staff to work harder and longer. These pressure points, though, are watershed moments for organizations. I've seen some leaders go to their staff, explain the difficult situation they're in, and say something like, "I know I'm asking for a lot, but here's what I need you to do. I'm in it with you, and together, we'll get through this." In these cases, the vast majority of staff members respond by rolling up their sleeves and working tirelessly, and the experience builds the bond between them and the leadership team. But too often, I've been called in after the leader damaged people and eroded their trust in him by simply demanding "more bricks with less straw"—a sure recipe for resentful staff!

Leaders may communicate unrealistic expectations in any area: deadlines, workload, skills, training, communication, or productivity. In dysfunctional cultures, however, any question from an employee is met by an angry response: "I don't care what it takes. Just get it done!"

BLAMING OTHERS

Most of us have no idea how much it means to our staff when we take responsibility for our blunders. Almost nothing builds trust like a leader's accepting responsibility, and almost nothing destroys it as quickly as blaming others for one's mistakes.

FEELING THREATENED BY OTHERS' SUCCESS

Some leaders desperately want to appear supremely confident but actually are terribly insecure. They demand to be the center of attention, the go-to person for the organization, and they feel threatened when anyone else succeeds or receives applause. These leaders may occasionally smile and pat successful people on the back because they know it's expected of them, but perceptive staff can tell that their smile hides a grimace.

POWER STRUGGLES

When organizations don't enjoy an atmosphere of trust and respect, they quickly degenerate into a law of the jungle and survival of the fittest mind-set. Fitness, in toxic cultures, is measured not by competence but by cunning. In these organizations, people often form alliances—just as contestants do on the reality show *Survivor*. People secretly plot against each other, forming secret (or not so secret) alliances. Gossip, deception, lies, and sabotage become chess pieces in the game. In the end, everyone loses, even those who thought they won, because those who watched them as well as those who participated lost respect for people playing the game.

DISHONESTY

Some leaders may be able to fool some of the people some of the time, but they can't fool all the people all the time. Sooner or later, their dishonesty will come back to bite them. People treasure truth, fairness, and justice, so deceptive leaders shatter their reputations, breaking trust with those whom they need most to run a successful organization.

CREATING AN ATMOSPHERE OF FEAR

Fear is one of the most powerful motivators in the world—and one of the most destructive. The reason so many leaders use it is that it's very effective, and when these leaders see how it controls people's behavior, the effect is almost addictive. Harsh words and deeds don't have to happen every day to destroy a ministry environment. Even occasional outbursts of anger and condemnation stick in the minds and hearts of the staff to create the fear that such outbursts could happen again—and could happen to them!

Angry leaders soon become convinced that fear works very well as a motivational tool, and they close their eyes to the damage they cause. Soon it becomes a normal part of the organization's culture. Leaders who use fear to control people, however, need to remember that there are other, better ways to motivate people.

USING PEOPLE INSTEAD OF VALUING THEM

Do you think people can tell if their leaders value them or are just using them for their own selfish ends? A few unperceptive staff members may not be able to tell, or they may be so happy to have a job that they're willing to put up with it, but most of them inherently resent being seen as things instead of people.

UNCLEAR VISION, STRATEGY, GOALS, AND VALUES

People don't thrive in confusion. When a leader charts a clear course, the staff may ask a lot of questions before they get on board, and some may drag their feet for a long time before they embrace the skipper's map, but understanding is an essential element of a healthy work environment. Some leaders don't invite questions when they make their pronouncement of the future. Maybe they're not too sure about it themselves. And a few leaders believe that a slick presentation should wow people enough that they won't have any questions at all. A clear grasp of the direction of the organization, though, is essential for there to be alignment and teamwork in each area of ministry. Without it, people wander, complain, doubt their leaders, chart their own course, or leave to find better leaders. Unpredictable leaders produce tentative followers.

A LACK OF AUTHENTICITY

People thrive on genuine appreciation, but they bristle when they sense that affirmations are less than sincere. A staff member of a megachurch told me, "I wish the ministry director wouldn't ever try to compliment me. Every time he does, it seems so contrived, forced, and insincere. I'd much rather hear nothing than that." It's not enough for leaders simply to say the right things; their people have to believe that in the depths of their hearts, the leaders mean them—and they shouldn't say them until and unless their words can be genuine.

People around us can sense when we're being sincere and when we're phony. They despise phoniness, but they thrive on sincere appreciation, even if it's not as frequent or as eloquent as they'd like it to be. A lack of authenticity in appreciation further erodes trust and creates doubt among the troops.

Very few senior leaders of toxic environments read books like this. The last thing they want is an objective appraisal of the dysfunction in their organizations. However, a few find the courage to make drastic changes. And top leaders across the rest of the spectrum long for their churches and nonprofits to be strong, healthy places where people thrive, support each other, and celebrate each other's successes. That, they are convinced, is the key to genuine success for their organizations, their leadership teams, their staff members, and those they serve. They have learned to be wary of the culture killers and address them quickly when their ugly heads arise.

CHAPTER 3
SEVEN KEYS OF CULTURE

To look at something as though we had never seen it before requires great courage. —HENRI MATISSE, PAINTER

A MAZINGLY, SOME OF US WHO are incredibly perceptive about other cultures are clueless about the nature of relationships and attitudes around us each day. To be objective, we need to step back from time to time and take a good, long look in the mirror. We might be surprised at what we see.

People have an almost limitless capacity for self-deception. We don't know what we don't know and are therefore unconsciously incompetent. If we were aware of our deficits, we'd ask questions and find solutions, but because we're not aware, we stay stuck in the status quo until something shakes us awake.

Quite often, we need some help to see things clearly. We are simply too close to the people and systems in our own environment to be objective.

BEYOND EXCUSES

When I talk with leaders and teams about creating a new culture, many of them instantly realize the beauty and power of working together in an inspiring environment, and they commit themselves to do whatever it takes to achieve it. Others, however, find creative excuses for remaining stuck in the past.

Analyzing a team's culture is a lot like marriage counseling. The way people relate to each other and the way things get done are entrenched patterns that have been in place for years. These patterns frustrate people, but nobody talks about them until someone from the outside addresses the core issues of culture, connection, and communication. When I consult with pastors and teams, I often begin by asking, "Imagine your team is the U.S. Congress. How does a bill get passed here?" Quite often, people roll their eyes or laugh in a passive-aggressive way. They feel uncomfortable because I've asked a question that addresses more than surface issues.

To help the team members uncover their needs and desires, I often ask, "If the meeting ended right now and you could make one suggestion to the pastor (or team leader) to improve the church or the team, what would it be? Anything goes. What would you suggest to him?" Recently, when I asked this question in a team, the responses included,

1. "Better strategic planning."

2. "Implement what we plan instead of just leaving the plans on a piece of paper."

3. "Clear communication and coordination." "Empower people to do what they're asked to do." "Simplify the strategy."

4. "Add strength and value to the present team." "Relax more and enjoy what we do."

5. "Clear and simple opportunities to engage the vision." "Hold people accountable."

6. "Plan ahead, and include us in the planning." "Celebrate our achievements."

7. "Stop changing the goalposts."

Their answers told me volumes about their culture. These suggestions surfaced their perceptions of their current environment. Without saying, "Pastor, I don't feel valued by you, and I'm afraid you're going to replace me with someone else," the person communicated the same idea by suggesting that the pastor "value the present team." Words matter, and they often carry multiple meanings.

Pastors and team leaders genuinely want to be the best leaders they can be. When the issue of culture is raised, they simply haven't known the right questions to ask to get below the surface to talk about the team's environment. When I ask these questions and pastors hear their staff members' responses, they are often surprised, but they always want to talk more about their perceptions. Insight provides choices, and these choices become steps in creating a vibrant culture.

Pastors and business leaders report that it's relatively easy to institute a new program or introduce a new product, but changing the culture is the hardest thing they've ever done. It requires wisdom, courage, and tenacity, but it begins with an understanding of the current condition.

A GLIMPSE OF THE CULTURE

I want to invite you and your team to look in the mirror to see the nature of your culture. The categories of "healthy" and "unhealthy" aren't very helpful because they aren't specific. To go deeper, we'll examine seven important factors that shape organizational culture, and for each of these, we'll identify particular attitudes and behaviors that point a culture toward either inspiration or toxicity. As we examine these, don't focus on yourself. Instead, take the temperature of your whole team. Culture is about relationships, communication, and shared values, not just about an individual's perceptions and behavior.

CONTROL

People function most effectively if they are given control (or authority) with responsibility. If they are held accountable for a task without having the means to accomplish it, they'll fail, and they'll be terribly frustrated.

On the other end of the spectrum, if control is concentrated in one person who insists on making virtually all important decisions, the organization experiences a significant bottleneck. It should be a warning if everyone is expected to consult with one person about everything before moving on. Teams thrive when there is a free flow of information and ready access to resources.

Contrary to the beliefs of some people, *control* isn't a dirty word. Delegating responsibility and maintaining accountability are essential for any organization to be effective. Strong, effective teams have a "Goldilocks approach" to control: not too much, not too little, but just the right amount of checks and balances. The leader gives clear direction, assigns tasks, delegates authority, provides resources, and then has a reasonable reporting procedure so the person can provide updates, coordinate with others, and stay on track until the task is finished.

Quite often, the real power broker on a team isn't the person at the head of the table. Good leaders involve everyone in the planning process, but sometimes an angry, sour, or demanding person can dominate a team. A sure sign of problems with control on a team are turf issues. When two or more people believe they have responsibility and authority for a task, they compete with each other for resources and, even more, for supremacy over each other.

Team members need to see themselves as partners in a grand venture, not competing for control over others, not carving out territory to defend to the death, but using delegated authority for the common good.

UNDERSTANDING

Every person on a team needs to have a clear grasp of the vision, his or her role, the gifts and contributions of the team members, and the way the team functions. Each person should be able to clearly articulate each of these vital aspects of the team's life.

The vision must be both global and specific—too big for anyone to accomplish without the power of God, but with handles on each person's specific role in fulfilling aspects of the overall vision. It breaks my heart when I talk to a staff member who says glumly, "I'm not really sure what I'm doing here."

Team communications are everybody's responsibility. Certainly the leader's task is to make sure each person clearly grasps the principles and delegated tasks, but good teams normalize the question everyone can ask: "Would you explain that again? I'm not sure I got it." In this way, misunderstanding is never an excuse for not getting the job done. Similarly, before a meeting is over, the leader can ask each person to share priorities, schedule, and coordination needed with other team members. This way, everyone is on the same page.

Understanding, though, isn't just about the *what* of ministry; it's also about the *why*. Again, grasping the underlying concepts is everybody's job. Leaders need to take time to explain how a new program fits into the plan, why it will make a difference in people's lives, and the important role each person will play in making it successful.

LEADERSHIP

Healthy teams are pipelines of leadership development. They recognize that an organization is only as healthy as the pool of rising leaders, so they actively seek to *discover* those who show leadership potential, *develop* resources to equip and inspire leaders, and carefully *deploy* them in roles that enflame their hearts, challenge them to excel, and propel the organization to new heights.

We need to make a distinction between leadership and management. To develop people to become leaders, we focus on heart and character. Training is important, but it's a management issue, equipping people to perform a particular task. Both are significant, but developing people is far more essential in creating a healthy culture than training people in specific skills. Plenty of toxic and discouraging cultures have highly trained, efficient staff members. They know how to do their jobs very well, but their culture stinks.

Many church teams focus on training people to accomplish tasks, but they neglect the essential role of developing leaders. In many cases, staff members are under enormous stress. They have a long list of jobs that need to be done—and done now!—and they're desperate for help. They are thrilled and relieved when someone steps into the gap to complete a task, but they don't even think about developing the person as a leader. We'll never have truly healthy cultures, however, if we don't identify and develop a host of strong, creative, passionate leaders.

Team leaders need to be perceptive about how rising leaders are assimilated into the group. Are old leaders threatened, or do they celebrate and mentor the new people? Great organizations enlist existing leaders to be part of the leadership pipeline, encouraging them to offer their insights and expertise and to help young leaders in every possible way.

TRUST

Mutual trust among team members is the glue that makes everything good possible. Without it, a team quickly disintegrates into a gang of people protecting their turf and forming angry alliances. When people trust each other, they make a strong connection between the vision, their own roles, the input of others, strategic planning, and the steps of implementation.

Trust may be freely given, but it is usually earned as people watch each other respond in good times and bad. Integrity and consistency provide a firm foundation for relationships to thrive. Trust is fluid. It takes time to be built, but it can be destroyed in an instant. Trust can be shattered in an instant by a dramatic event, or, more often, it is slowly eroded by countless relatively small but abrasive comments and actions. Every team is made up of flawed human beings, so on every team, trust will be an issue to some degree at some time with someone. Depending on the situation, it doesn't have to ruin a team. In fact, relationships that rebuild broken trust often are stronger and healthier than ever before because the people involved had to be ruthlessly honest, find forgiveness, and communicate better than before.

UNAFRAID

Corporate courage is an incredibly appealing but slippery trait. Church teams aren't fighting a battle against flesh and blood, but men and women on staff teams face difficulties and challenges with courage if, and only if, they are convinced that what they are doing counts for all eternity and they believe in the people serving on their team.

Healthy teams foster the perspective that failure isn't a tragedy and conflict isn't the end of the world. Great leaders welcome dissenting opinions, as long as they are offered in good will and with an eye toward a solution. These teams are willing to take great risks and even to fail miserably because they've gotten over the notion that failure is a personal flaw.

They believe that God is worthy of noble efforts, and they trust that God smiles on them as they attempt great things for him. When they look at one another, they don't see competitors; they see friends who have their backs as they take big risks. Courage, support, and innovation go hand in hand in inspiring cultures.

RESPONSIVE

Teams with healthy cultures are alert to open doors and ones that are closing. An individual may not notice a particular threat or opportunity, but someone else on the team will. These teams develop the productive habit of keeping their eyes open so that they can handle every situation: on the team, in individuals' lives, in the church family, and in the community.

For teams to be responsive, they have to develop a consistent process for collaboration, with communication lines that are wide open. They value analysis and feedback, and they work on becoming and staying aligned with one another. Responsive teams don't just focus on big goals and sweeping strategies. They develop the habit of taking care of the little things, such as promptly returning phone calls, responding to e-mails, and communicating decisions to everyone who needs to know when he or she needs to know it.

Leaders in healthy cultures work hard to disseminate information among the departments and get buy-in up and down the chain of command and between teams. Being responsive requires both a sensitive spirit and a workable system to make sure things don't fall through the cracks. The larger the organization grows, the greater the amount of energy that needs to be invested in being responsive to people inside and outside the team.

EXECUTION

In my conversations with leaders and team members, one of their chief concerns is that teams often talk about decisions but fail to follow through on implementing them. When they don't see the fruit of their discussions, they lose faith in each other and become discouraged. Executing decisions is a function of clarity, roles and responsibilities, and the system of accountability.

To be sure that follow-through becomes the norm, leaders need to define goals very clearly. Decisions should be articulated with precision, including who, what, why, when, where, and how. Clear delegation is essential to execution. The person responsible needs to understand her authority and how to relate to everyone else involved. This person should walk out of the meeting with crystal-clear expectations, a plan to coordinate with others, deadlines, and any other requirements.

On some teams, accountability is haphazard at best, but this breeds complacency even among those who would normally be conscientious about following through with their commitments. People don't do what we expect; they do what we inspect. Plans are worthless unless they have target goals, deadlines, access to resources, and a budget. With those things in place, the leader needs to ask for regular updates on progress. She can ask in any way that works: e-mail, phone calls, personal appointments, or, even better, in the staff meetings. Some people mistakenly believe that deadlines aren't very important, but they are the benchmark that keeps a plan on track.

Developing a culture of accountability takes the mystery and the sting out of giving reports. If everybody is asked to report, then nobody is singled out. In a culture that executes plans well, the leader is committed to ongoing training to equip team members to achieve the highest goals.

GETTING BUY-IN

One person can change the composition of a team. It's best if the leader grasps the importance of creating an inspiring culture and takes bold steps with the team, but a wise, tenacious team member can begin to create this kind of environment.

I've seen some leaders try to change their organizations by fiat, demanding that people trust each other, communicate freely, and be more responsive to those inside and outside the team. But as you can imagine, these efforts only further eroded the environment and created one more hurdle to overcome. Great leaders put cultural issues on the table and invite honest, open, and transparent conversations about changing the atmosphere. They know it's going to take time, and they are willing to lead the process. Building a great team involves everybody, and in fact it works most effectively when team members feel empowered to give input, develop strategies, and take steps in shaping the culture.

Changing a culture requires tremendous patience. We can rearrange boxes on an organizational chart in a moment, but changing culture is heart surgery. Culture is not only *what* we do but also *why* and *how* we do it. Culture is about the heart and head, and then it shapes what we do with our hands. Leaders also need a healthy dose of creativity as they take their teams through cultural change.

Cultural transformation may begin when an individual has a fresh insight about the need to work together more effectively, but sooner or later, everyone on the team has to get involved in the process. Some jump on the wagon with enthusiasm; others are brought along more reluctantly—but everyone on the team has to become a willing partner in the venture. When people bring their best to the team, amazing things can happen. As the Japanese proverb says, "None of us is as smart as all of us."

CHAPTER 4
VOCABULARY DEFINES CULTURE

When you have healthy supervisors and good working conditions, what more do workers look for?... There is really only one answer to this question: Recognition. Not just bonuses and plaques, privileged parking spaces or "worker of the week" announcements, though these are very important, but the type of recognition that affirms the value of your self at the deepest possible level. —DR. ARCHIBALD HART

WORDS HAVE THE POWER TO shape lives and organizations. Too often, however, leaders aren't aware of their vocabulary as they speak, and they don't realize how people are affected by their words. Even casually spoken statements can have profound effects. The words we use, and the way we use them, define organizational culture. Some leaders think that the vocabulary of culture is only about painting the biggest, most dramatic vision they can paint—the bigger the better. But that's not the case. Vision statements are only a small part of the vocabulary of a culture. Factors that are just as important include

1. Avoiding terms that actually hinder us from fulfilling God's vision

2. Using informal, compassionate conversations to show empathy and build trust

3. Occasionally stopping in the middle of a meeting to talk about how the team is communicating

4. Being honest with team members and avoiding "happy talk"

5. Learning to listen with our hearts, eyes, and ears

6. Speaking words of genuine affirmation

7. Intentionally choosing vocabulary to shape the culture

For most of us, the words we use are second nature. We don't even think about them anymore, but we can't overestimate the power of vocabulary to define culture. To make changes, we need honest reflection, feedback from the stakeholders at every level, and the courage to change not only our words but also our hearts as we speak them.

EVERY INDUSTRY HAS A VOCABULARY

Every field of study, every industry, and every organization creates its own vocabulary to communicate to its constituents. Insiders instantly recognize the meaning of words that may sound like a foreign language to outsiders. And in some fields, such as technology, vocabulary is changing at a rapid pace. Our choice of words creates a bond among those who understand the meanings and context, but it also builds walls that keep out those who don't understand.

Vocabulary makes a difference in communicating at every level of a church's life: one-on-one, in teams, in departments, churchwide, and to the community. Too often, our language becomes exclusive—and even offensive—to people in the community we are trying to reach with the message of Christ. The existing vocabulary in a church is seldom analyzed—and even less often challenged—because the choice of terms is ritualized in an airtight tradition. Many churches still use the same vocabulary they used decades (and even generations) ago, and as the culture changes around us, we sound increasingly irrelevant.

THE LANGUAGE OF TRUST

Trust is the glue of any relationship, and authenticity is essential. When people get too busy to care for one another, trust erodes and defenses go up. Even though we are trying to reach every person on the planet, we need to slow down to show interest in each individual. When ministry leaders forget that their staff members are flesh-and-blood human beings and treat them as "production units," these leaders lose their voice to speak vision, direction, and challenge into others' lives. Small talk about the things that matter to people on our teams isn't small at all—it's enormously important.

Most pastors enter the ministry because they love people, and they are gifted at the art of chitchat. They can talk to almost anybody at almost any time about almost anything. As the pressures of ministry compound, however, they tend to focus more on the administrative load and looming deadlines. Then every interaction becomes an organizational transaction instead of a relational connection.

Trust is built when we use inclusive instead of exclusive language: "I" instead of "you," "us" instead of "them," and "we" instead of "they." Obviously, sometimes we have to use words like "you," "them," and "they," but we need to watch the context and nuance of the message. For example, I've been in a staff meeting when someone said, "After *we* make this decision, *we* have to make sure that *they* understand what it means." The subtle implication was that the people in the room were the insiders and everyone else was an outsider. A better statement would be, "After this decision is made, we have to be sure that the whole team understands the implications." This wording implies that everyone is on the team, with equal value and equal status.

As staff teams grow larger with multiple layers of leadership, I'm afraid that some churches are losing some of the magic of the vocabulary of volunteers. In the business community and with paid staff, we feel that we can demand compliance because people pick up a paycheck every couple of weeks. Sadly, too many churches treat volunteers like paid staff and demand compliance with precious little heart motivation. Instead, we need to treat staff like volunteers, always appealing to their hearts and their desire for God to use them to change lives.

The culture of a team is shaped by the dominant person, who may not necessarily be the one with the title who sits at the head of the table. This person may be an enthusiastic, charismatic team member who expresses optimism that the team can accomplish even the most difficult challenge, but more often, it's a surly, opinionated person who feels compelled to voice every objection under the sun. The dominant person either demands to be the power broker or steps into a void left by an ineffective leader. Soon, the vocabulary used by the dominant person becomes the collective language of the team. Notice how each person promotes his or her issue, and observe the response of the team members.

STARTING STRONG

The first thirty to forty-five seconds of a meeting are crucial. Most leaders, however, don't think much about how people are introduced to the meeting and the message of the day. When we sit down at a conference table, the people in the room don't give us much more time than a few seconds. If we don't grab their hearts in those first few seconds, their minds will drift to other things they have quickly concluded are more important than our less-than-compelling agenda. And again, vocabulary is important. I've walked into a meeting when the leader announced, "I'm not sure what we need to do today," and the disinterest in the room was almost palpable. I've also heard a leader begin a meeting by saying, "A lot of people have told me that they disagreed with our decision." Immediately, I realized I had to guess who he was talking about, and I didn't want to play a guessing game. I wanted the cold, hard facts, with the issue stated as a challenge the team could overcome as they marshal their collective resources to meet it. A better way to begin the meeting is to say, "Last Thursday, I met with Larry (who, everyone knows, is a major donor), and he has some questions about the direction of the youth ministry." I may not agree with Larry's assessment of the situation, but I respect Larry as a key member of the church. The vocabulary used in this first sentence captures my attention and piques my interest.

As leaders we need to carefully plan the first couple of sentences for every meeting we lead. Very simply, a good beginning can say something like, "What we are talking about in this meeting has implications for the way the community perceives our church (or how we develop leaders, or anything else that's important to the team). This meeting is crucial, and we need everyone's help." Make the first statement positive instead of negative, inclusive instead of exclusive, and hopeful instead of complaining about the past. A few minutes of preparation equip us to begin well, and those first moments work wonders to grab people's hearts and set the tone for the rest of the meeting.

ASIDES

As we prepare for meetings and carefully choose our vocabulary for the first few sentences, we can anticipate who on the team will be the "yes, but" people and who will be the "yes, and" people. One of our jobs as leaders is to give some power to those who will carry the ball down the field and to gently nudge the negative people to see problems as challenges. Identifying these people doesn't take a doctorate in psychology. We've seen team members respond in dozens of meetings before, and we can accurately predict how they'll respond this time.

A leader's feedback about team members' contributions in a meeting is just as important as the discussion itself. These brief interludes and reflections are "asides" that guide group members' perceptions of how they are working together. In many meetings, I stop and reflect on a person who has made a valuable contribution. I may say something to the group like, "Did you notice what just happened in our discussion?" Then I'll turn to the individual and say, "Bill, you helped us move the conversation forward when you asked an insightful question, listened carefully, and then offered a solution. Could you tell how your contribution affected our meeting? I sure noticed, and I want you to know that I appreciate your impact today."

Sometimes, honest feedback can serve the dual purposes of correction and inspiration. When I noticed that Mary was always voicing concerns and shooting down constructive ideas, I stopped the meeting and said, "Mary, let me give you some feedback about how you influence the group. I've noticed that you have very good insights about the challenges we face, and you articulate them very well, but I haven't seen you offer many constructive solutions. That's important, too." Then I turn to the team and tell them, "Let's make this a standard for our team: let's be very frank about the challenges we face, but when we bring up something in the group, let's also offer at least three possible solutions to discuss. And now, let's get back to the point we were discussing." Mary knows that I haven't targeted her behavior alone for correction; we've made a commitment as a team to be rigorously honest and solution oriented. The mesage to the group is that the leader is aware not only of the issue being discussed but also of the way each group member is framing that issue. The process of the conversation is just as important (and ultimately, even more important) than the immediate topic of the conversation.

THE GIFT OF HONESTY

One of the most valuable things we can give people on our teams is the gift of honesty. People instinctively know if a leader is holding back information, shading the truth, or expressing blind optimism. Happy talk may be intended to look like genuine faith in God, but it comes across as phony, and a lack of authenticity poisons a team. The beginning point, though, isn't for the leader to simply analyze word choices. It's deeper than that. The first task is to take a long, hard look at the difference between respecting people and manipulating them. The two are polar opposites. When we respect someone, we value her as a person, and we honor her opinions even if we disagree with her. When a leader's agenda is to control people to get them to believe "the right way" and do "the right things," he's engaged in manipulation, not true leadership.

The gift of honesty begins not with words but with the leader's perception and intentions. When we feel stressed, threatened, or out of control, our instinctive response is "fight or flight." We become defensive and demanding, and our goal changes from leading people to controlling them. In a flash or over a long period, we shift from treating them like adults to treating them like small children. When we play the role of "benevolent parents," we feel justified in telling them only part of the truth, and we protect our position as the keepers of reality. We may have seen people on our teams worry or explode when they learned painful information, and we want to avoid that response again at all costs—perhaps because we interpret their negative response as a reflection on our leadership. First, then, we need to be honest with ourselves about how we view people on our teams. Do we respect them as adults and thus can be honest with them, or do we believe we need to treat them like children and filter the information we share with them?

Authenticity requires another step, however. If we want to create a culture of trust on our teams, leaders also need to acknowledge any personal faults in communicating with the team and the harm they have done. One ministry leader told his team, "During the last few months when we've been under a lot of stress with the reorganization, I realized I haven't been the leader you need me to be. Instead of treating you like adults and telling you the truth, I've hidden some things from you. I think you sensed that, and I can tell that you don't trust me as much as you used to. I take responsibility for that, and I'm sorry. I can give lots of excuses, but good intentions aren't good enough. Will you forgive me?" After they responded, he continued, "I promise I'll do whatever it takes for us to have healthy relationships, and I'll tell you the truth. I want you to be a part of the solution, and if I don't tell you the truth, you can't be. What do you think about what I've said today?"

His last question invited people on the team to share their frustration, anger, and disappointment. The leader may not want to hear these comments, but they are the path of healing and hope for the future of the team. When team members share their hearts, especially hurtful things, the leader needs to listen carefully without a shred of defensiveness. One of the most important statements a leader can make during these conversations is actually a question: "Would you tell me more about that?" This simple question shows that he welcomes the team member's honest feedback.

When people have shared their frustrations and the tank of disappointment has run dry, the leader can express hope that the future will be different. His commitment is, "From now on, I'll treat you with respect. I promise. And if you ever feel that I'm trying to manipulate you, I give you permission to tell me. I assure you that I'll listen. Can we make that commitment to each other?" The leader's promise and invitation provide a strong foundation for the future of the team, but the original organizational challenge hasn't gone away. It's still a steep hill for the team to climb. The leader needs to state the challenge objectively, without promising "everything will work out just fine." That's just happy talk. A more accurate and more reassuring statement would be, "We face a tough challenge, but I'm sure God has some purposes in it for all of us. Let's tackle it together."

To make sure there are no hidden agendas and unaddressed emotional baggage, I developed a habit of ending meetings by going around the room and asking each person, "Is there anything you haven't said to me that you need to say or want to say?" Sometimes people seize the opportunity to say, "Yes, I have a concern that I want you to know about." And we take some time to address it there. The vocabulary of honesty can be spoken only by a leader who has made a commitment to respect people on the team.

Manipulation, even with the best of intentions, may bring short-term gains of lowering tension for the moment, but it eventually causes people to feel devalued, and they conclude that the leader isn't a person they want to follow. Respect, honesty, responsibility, and hope are the language of a great team leader.

QUESTIONS AND SLOUCHING

Never in all of history has communication been so immediate and accessible, but I'm afraid the technological advances have had the unintended consequence of eroding the art of listening. The proliferation of devices has changed the way we relate. We expect to stay connected to everyone and everything through our cell phones, PDAs, text messaging, e-mail, and the Internet. To change the way we communicate with people so that we genuinely connect with them instead of just passing on information, we can do two simple but profound things to enhance listening: ask pertinent questions and use the power of slouching. People get tired in meetings if they feel that they're being *talked to* but not invited to *talk with* the rest of the team.

Asking for additional input takes a little longer, but we have to understand the goal of our meetings. If the goal is to check off all the boxes on an arbitrary list of items, then by all means, press forward and charge through the list. But if the goal is to enflame the hearts of people and enlist their passionate involvement in the process, then we need to slow down and involve them more deeply in the conversation by asking for their contributions. Of course, taking time to ask for input, listen carefully, and value discussion about a finite list of topics doesn't leave time for other things that could have been discussed. The leader's role is then to be the CPO, the chief priority officer. They need to know that we will address important topics, but we need to be flexible and prepared so that we use our time wisely. When individuals and teams are confident, they feel free to fully engage the situation and each other. I call this "dancing in the moment."

Many of us feel that we have to settle every disagreement before we can move on, so we avoid disagreements—especially with people who have a history of being sour or demanding. An important principle of creating a healthy culture is becoming comfortable with some unresolved issues. A leader can say, "I can tell that we disagree about this, and I don't think we're going to resolve it now. Let's think about it and talk again next week. I want to ask each of you to bring a possible solution when we talk again." With this mind-set, we can ask for input without demanding universal agreement and instant compliance.

Listening, though, isn't just about getting the facts. Nonverbal communication is very important, especially when we're listening. When I'm leading a team or meeting with an individual, I often employ "the power of slouching." I push my chair away from the table, sit back, cross my legs, and turn to face the person who is speaking so as to make eye contact. These actions send a powerful message: "I care about you and what you have to say, and I'm not in a hurry for you finish. Take your time and give me your best input." Giving people our undivided, relaxed attention lets them know that we are listening with our minds, our hearts, and our eyes, as well as with our ears. They feel that they are important and that we value them as people, not just as interchangeable cogs in the organizational machine.

"SOME PEOPLE"

One of the guidelines in building authentic relationships is to avoid vague accusations. Years ago, I spent far too much time chasing rabbits when someone in a group reported, "*Some people* have a problem with this or that." We tried to guess who it was, and we tried to address the problem even though the person who reported it was intentionally vague to protect his sources. Fairly soon, I realized this had to change, so I told the group, "We won't bring up any reports or complaints unless we identify the person who told us. If you don't have the person's permission to tell us, then don't make the report." I don't read anonymous letters. I tear them up and discard them. Anonymous people are cowards.

The principle of dealing with specifics instead of vague generalities also applies to how team members talk about the leader. People talk about their leaders—it's human nature—but they need to be taught that authenticity works both ways. They need to speak honestly with their leaders if they have concerns about their leadership.

CONSISTENCY

People on staff and volunteer teams watch their leaders like a hawk, and they want to see consistency between their words and their actions. A friend of mine told me about the leader of a national ministry who presented himself as a kind, wise, compassionate man of God, but behind closed doors, he was demanding and severely critical of anyone who dared voice a dissenting view. Soon his staff members were divided into the loyalists who turned a blind eye to his incongruent behavior, and the dissenters whose frustration and disrespect created enormous tension in their own lives and their relationships in the organization. I've also known a few leaders whose public and private personas were reversed. They were as kind and loving as a mother with the people in their offices and boardrooms, but when they spoke to the masses, they conveyed a raw anger that seemed far more than a righteous response to injustice.

As Abraham Lincoln famously said, "You can fool all of the people some of the time, and some of the people all of the time, but you can't fool all the people all the time." Followers notice the consistency of a leader's life. If his attitudes and behaviors in private match his public words of faith and nobility, they know they can trust him. If not, they first lose respect for the leader, then for their coworkers who remain loyal, and, finally, even for themselves for staying in such a toxic culture.

Thankfully, cases of significant inconsistency in churches and nonprofit organizations are fairly rare. The ones that make the news capture our attention, but for every one of those, there are thousands of churches with competent, consistent leaders. To some degree, all leaders struggle with consistency because they have to balance vision for the future with compassion today for hurting people, but most find a way to live successfully in that tension. It's a wonderful thing when people report, "He's the same person in the lobby that he is in the pulpit, and he's the same in the committee meeting as he is in the hardware store." People thrive under this kind of leadership. Loyalty earned is a beautiful thing, but loyalty demanded is toxic.

AUTHENTIC AFFIRMATION

When my friend told me years ago that he saw me as a "really good leader," his message was powerful because I could tell he meant it. For words of affirmation to be meaningful, they need to be specific, personal, and timely. I've heard many leaders say to almost anyone within earshot, "You're great!" That's a lot better than "I hate your guts," but global comments seldom yield significant results. Affirming someone's character or abilities is a skill that requires preparation and practice. It's easy, especially for verbal communicators, to become lazy in their praise of people. Instead, they need to think carefully about the people they lead, and then notice, name, and nurture the characteristics they value. Instead of saying to a volunteer, "Man, you're terrific," it's much more meaningful for a leader to think about that person, the obstacles he has overcome, and how God is using him in specific ways—the more descriptive, the better. Then, in a private moment or in a meeting, the leader might say, "Sean, I've been watching you, and I'm really impressed with how you care for people. You consistently go out of your way. I saw you take extra time with Mrs. Adams when she couldn't get the answer she needed and she was getting frustrated. She really appreciated your help, and I want you to know that I appreciate you, too."

There's no magic formula for authentic affirmation. We can focus on a pattern of behavior or praise a single event we noticed. We might point out character qualities like compassion, courage, or persistence, or we can focus on skills of administration or leadership. The most important element of affirming someone is that she realizes we've been thinking about her, and our comments aren't "out of the blue." There's certainly nothing wrong with spontaneous praise for people we lead, but praise is even more powerful when they are convinced that we have been watching and admiring them for a while. If we say too much too often, people discount what we say, and if we don't say enough, they wonder what we really think about them. We need a balanced approach to words of affirmation: not too seldom, not too often, but just the right amount at the right time.

A CLOSER LOOK

How can we tell if our vocabulary is defining the culture we desire? We can pay attention to the signals we receive from the people around us, especially those closest to us. When their signals confuse us, we need to give ourselves permission to ask questions like, "What's going on? The people out there respond very well to my leadership, but those close to me look frustrated. Maybe I need to take a look at my words, my nonverbals, my congruence, and my authenticity." Feeling confused about our leadership isn't a bad thing. It's often the first step toward deeper analysis and change.

Changing culture always creates conflict. When we choose respect instead of manipulation, and honesty instead of avoidance of issues, most people will thrive, but a few resist even healthy changes. Don't be surprised when people on your team feel uncomfortable with honesty. Give them time to adjust, and keep loving them as you model a new vocabulary, but realize that some people may not want to participate in the new culture. They felt comfortable, and perhaps powerful, in the old one, and they prefer things to stay the way they were.

Our vocabulary, and especially the tone we use when we speak, powerfully defines and reflects culture. It's very easy to keep saying the same things in the same way over and over again, and expect different results—but that's a definition of insanity, not leadership. Unexamined vocabulary puts a ceiling on leadership.

CHAPTER 5
CHANGE STARTS WITH ME

It's amazing how someone's IQ seems to double as soon as you give them responsibility and indicate that you trust them. — TIMOTHY FERRISS

SOME OF US HAVE EXCEPTIONALLY high expectations of the leaders and the organization where we serve. Unrealistically high expectations cloud our perspective, create unwarranted disappointment, and steal our emotional energy. Certainly, some cultures are so toxic that the best course is to leave as quickly and as graciously as possible, but far more often, the best place to start a revolution of change is in our own hearts and minds. Instead of waiting for the top leader to change the culture and make everything smooth, pleasant, and easy, we need to begin with the one person we have the power to control: ourselves.

REPLACING DISAPPOINTMENT

Christians, and especially those who serve in visionary churches, often have incredibly high expectations of their leaders. They may have come from painful past situations in a family or church environment, and they hope, "This time, it'll be different!" They read glowing accounts of other churches, and they see how Jesus invited his followers to experience his love.

They hope, pray, and expect—and too often demand—that this leader, this church, and this team will be heaven on earth. Expectations surface in vocabulary. A word that appears in their conversations and thoughts is "should," as in, "The pastor should do this or that better," "He should lead this way or that way," "The board should give me more authority," and countless others. The number of "shoulds" in a person's mind and mouth is inversely proportional to his sense of peace, joy, and fulfillment.

To replace any nagging disappointment created by unrealistic expectations, let me suggest a few strategies:

- Focus on what you can control.
- Be tenaciously thankful.
- Resolve any role alignment issues.
- Invest creative capital.

FOCUS ON WHAT YOU CAN CONTROL

Many of us expend enormous amounts of energy worrying about and trying to manage things that are outside the realm of our control. To maintain mental and emotional health, and to be the kind of leaders and team members we can be, we have to realize that we aren't God. The scope of our responsibility and power is limited, and we need to devote our energies to those things that are inside our sandboxes.

The first step, then, is for each of us to realize that we can't control the universe, or even the smaller universe of our church environment. For now, we need clear-eyed objectivity and optimism, with a commitment to do all we can to create a positive culture around us. Accepting responsibility for what we can control—and making a steadfast commitment not to complain about what's outside our control—are crucial ingredients in spiritual, emotional, and relational health.

BE TENACIOUSLY THANKFUL

Phillip had been missing out on much of the joy he could have been experiencing because his eyes had been riveted on the shortcomings of his senior pastor. It only took a few questions, though, for him to realize that God and his pastor had given him wonderful opportunities. His attitude almost immediately changed from griping to gratitude. From what I heard later, his thankful heart changed more than just his disposition. As the sludge of a critical spirit was washed away, he enjoyed his wife and family, his team, and every aspect of his ministry more than ever.

RESOLVE ANY ROLE ALIGNMENT ISSUES

Sometimes a person's disappointment with a leader or a team runs deeper than attitude. When the job description doesn't fit the person's gifts and interests, confusion and heartache inevitably occur. The challenge of finding the best fit in a culture isn't always easy to resolve, but it's essential for each person to find, not the perfect fit, but a "good enough fit" so that the individual, the team, and the mission work well together.

INVEST CREATIVE CAPITAL

In stagnant, discouraging, and toxic cultures, people spend their energies protecting themselves and creating alliances instead of creatively pursuing the mission. Even in accepting and inspiring cultures, individuals or pockets of people may live with deep disappointments caused by unrealistic expectations and shattered dreams. When people face these challenges with courage and hope, a new world opens up, and they can invest themselves in the cause that drew them there in the first place.

CHARACTERISTICS OF A CHANGE AGENT

Instead of waiting for the senior leaders or someone else to create a positive culture, each person on the team can take steps to be a change agent. Instead of waiting for someone to become trustworthy, each one can prove to be a trustworthy person; a man or woman of character, heart, and hope. There may be many different ways of describing people who, as leaders or team members, can shape organizational culture, including:

- Heart motivation
- Positive demeanor
- Courage to ask tough questions
- Honesty without limitations
- Warmth and humor
- Willingness to reflect reality

HEART MOTIVATION

One of the first things to realize is that staff members and volunteers in the church world are motivated by meaning, not money. Dangling financial incentives to entice them to work harder proves to be counterproductive. They don't want to perceive that they are being treated unfairly in regard to salaries, but to touch their deepest motivations, leaders need to appeal to their desire for their lives to count.

POSITIVE DEMEANOR

When the senior pastor says, "I believe God is calling us to trust him to pursue this vision," the atmosphere in the room is transformed if someone responds, "Pastor, we can trust God for that. Let's go for it." But a "can-do" spirit will only look like kissing up to the boss if another trait is missing . . .

COURAGE TO ASK TOUGH QUESTIONS

Change agents need to be positive, but they need to be multi-dimensional: they must also possess the ability to ask penetrating questions to help the group discern God's will, to find the best alignment of roles and goals, and to develop the best plan for any challenge.

HONESTY ABOUT LIMITATIONS

People who claim to be able to do everything well lose the trust of those around them. Change agents are unfailingly optimistic, but they also have a good grasp of their strengths and limitations. They are willing to say, "I can't do that very well, but I know someone who can." Being honest about holes in our skill set shows people that we aren't power hungry or driven to win approval. We notice others' strengths and affirm their contributions, and we gladly defer to them when they can do a job better than we can. In this way, everybody on the team feels valued.

WARMTH AND HUMOR

Every team needs someone who brings warmth to the relationships and can break the tension with humor from time to time. Remembering a birthday, a health concern, a child's struggle, or a joy in someone's life shows that we care about the people, not just the task they perform. Above all else, people want to know that others value them, and a word of warmth means everything to a team. And warmth is infectious. Just as one person's sour disposition can poison a team, an individual's sincere love for others can change the complexion of a meeting and a team.

WILLINGNESS TO REFLECT REALITY

Unhealthy teams never talk about "the elephant in the room." They dance around uncomfortable topics, even though avoiding them further erodes trust among the people on the team. At that point, the refusal to talk about the issues is a bigger deal than the issues themselves. People who are cultural change agents are willing to say, "This is what I see going on with this issue," and even, "This is what I see going on with our team right now." The first few times a leader practices healthy reflection, people on the team may feel uncomfortable simply because it's so novel. After a few times, though, team members realize that talking about "the process of processing" is essential to a healthy team culture.

PRACTICAL STEPS

For those of us who are serving in inspiring or accepting cultures, we simply want to sustain and enhance the quality of our relationships. Those who experience stagnant, discouraging, or toxic cultures, however, have more work to do to discover the right path forward. They may have been blasted for disagreeing with a leader, ignored and marginalized when they didn't measure up to the leader's expectations, or perhaps, even worse, patronized by insincere affirmations. In difficult cultures, people need to think clearly, avoid overreacting, and take wise steps. Let me offer a few suggestions:

- Go to the leader privately.
- Practice self-reflection.
- Make a commitment.
- Understand your equity and your risk tolerance.
- If you leave, go gracefully.

GO TO THE LEADER PRIVATELY

Never ever confront a senior leader publicly. It's a lose-lose-lose proposition. The leader gets angry because she loses face, you lose respect (and perhaps your job), and the culture goes backward because of escalating tension. No one likes to be told, "You're a bad leader" or "You're not doing that the right way." But most leaders will listen if a team member approaches them privately and with grace and wisdom, saying "I've been thinking about this, and I want to tell you my observations."

The title of this chapter is "Change Starts with Me." We don't want to communicate with a leader in a tone and using words that demand that he or she change—or else! When we come across in a condescending or demanding tone, we are hoping that change will start (and end) with the leader. It's far healthier for everybody if each team member accepts responsibility for his own behavior and learns to communicate respectfully and wisely with the leader and the rest of the team.

PRACTICE SELF-REFLECTION

Wise people notice dissonance in their emotions, thoughts, and relationships, and they take time to ask themselves, *What's that about?* As reflection becomes the habit of a lifetime, they are less surprised when they uncover selfish motives and harmful behaviors that may have been part of their lives since they were children.

Self-reflection is both planned and spontaneous. A question that I teach people to ask about themselves at regular intervals is, "What is it about *me* that keeps *me* from becoming the best *me* that God intended *me* to be?" This question invites us to take full responsibility for our growth and direction, and it rivets our purpose to God's plan for our lives. For leaders and team members, confusion about their hearts and their roles isn't the biggest problem they face. I believe the dissonance that comes from being responsive to the Spirit's prompting may be unsettling for a while, but it opens a door to insight, growth, and better connections with the people we love.

All of us need honest feedback from a spouse and close friends, but we need to be careful that we are asking for the truth, not lobbying for allies to defend us. Try approaching a few very close friends and asking, "Do you see any patterns that have surfaced lately in my attitudes and actions with the staff team? I think I've turned into a jerk. I've responded with anger over even little things. Have you seen that in me?" And they'll tell you what they've seen.

MAKE A COMMITMENT

Make a solemn commitment to be the best team member or leader you can be. Reflect on the attitude that has shaped your response, your skills in engaging your leader, and the impact you're having on others—and be honest with what you find. Think carefully about how to display the characteristics of a change agent, and take the risk to speak up, ask questions, offer encouragement, and be the kind of trustworthy person you want others to be.

Make a commitment to lead your own team with integrity, love, and skill. Be the kind of leader you want others to be. Even if you feel like a Lone Ranger, lead with passion and grace. As you lead your team, don't criticize your pastor or any other leaders in the church. And if your team members begin speaking negatively, stop them and explain how gossip ruins attitudes and relationships. God has a purpose for you as you lead your team. Look for him to lead you in every interaction with those you lead and with those on the team on which you serve as a member.

UNDERSTAND YOUR EQUITY AND YOUR RISK TOLERANCE

I've watched some staff members become angry or righteously indignant (depending on who's telling the story) and leave their position without thought of the implications to their families. I'm not advocating that anyone stay in a toxic, abusive environment one day longer than necessary, but you need to be aware of the consequences and timing of your choices.

To understand the context of your decision more fully, consider these questions:

• "Could I have misunderstood my leader?"

I've known spouses who have misinterpreted each other's behavior for many years, so it's certainly possible that you could have misunderstood the leader's words, actions, and especially motives.

• "How long has the problem been going on?"

If the difficulty with the leader has occurred only in the past few weeks, you need to be more patient and see if the problem vanishes as quickly as it appeared. Look for established patterns. Don't be too concerned about isolated blips on the radar. The severity and nature of the issue determine how patient you should be in trying to resolve it, cope with it, or confront it.

• "Am I oversensitive about defending my role or my department?"

Is the issue you are so upset about systemwide, or is it possible that a decision is being made for the good of the whole that seems unfair or inconsiderate to your department? Sometimes leaders make global decisions, but they don't explain them so that each department leader understands why the choice was made.

• "Do I have anywhere to go?"

It's not appropriate to use office hours to look for a position at a different church, unless of course you have permission from your team leader or pastor. I've seen men and women resign "on principle" with nowhere to go. If they had waited a little longer, they may have been able to make an exit more gracefully for everyone involved.

• "How does my decision affect my family?"

Decisions to resign in the heat of the moment seldom consider a spouse's employment or children's school situations. Consider the broader implications of the decision, not just how it makes you feel in your role and work relationships.

IF YOU LEAVE, GO GRACEFULLY

At some point, some of us will come to the conclusion that we can't be effective in the culture where we serve, and it's time to leave. If we have learned to live and serve with integrity and wisdom in a difficult culture, we will experience deep sadness for our own loss and for those who remain, because we care for them. However, if we haven't learned the lessons of being change agents, we'll either explode in anger or slink away in shame (or perhaps a combination of those painful emotions).

Here are a few guidelines for a graceful exit:

• Meet with the pastor and thank him for the opportunity to serve at the church. Explain that you believe God is leading you to serve at another church. Tell him that you want to make the transition to the next person as smooth as possible. Ask him what he wants you to do to make that happen (for example, related to teams, contact information with students, schedules, commitments for camps, and so on).

• When the pastor or others ask why you are leaving (and they will), don't use the moment as an opportunity to "clear the air" and blast the pastor and other leaders. Keep it pleasant, thankful, and future centered.

• The hardest conversations are often with the top volunteers, many of whom know the struggles and have great compassion for the person leaving. Don't let these conversations devolve into angry blaming sessions. Thank people for their hearts and their service, and celebrate all the things God has done through you as you served together.

- Pave the way for the new person by leaving everything in great shape.

We need to remember that God calls his church to unity, not uniformity. We don't all have to be the same for the body to work well, but we have to be committed to a common purpose—loving one another in spite of our differences and resolving disagreements agreeably.

HAPPINESS AND EFFECTIVENESS

In their thoughts and expectations, most people instinctively link happiness and effectiveness. They assume that the two are always mutually inclusive, but in observing people in hundreds of organizations, I can report that this isn't necessarily true. I've talked to people in stagnant and discouraging cultures, and even a few in toxic environments, who found a way to be effective in their work. They endured their team's passivity or pathology by putting their heads down and being the best they could be at the work God had given them to do. They weren't particularly happy, but they found a measure of satisfaction in "working heartily, as unto the Lord," and seeing lives changed. By contrast, I've not known anyone who was ineffective at the task she was commissioned to perform but found genuine joy on a team. God has made us so that we thrive emotionally at work only when we know we are contributing our knowledge and skills to accomplish something bigger than ourselves. Those who spend their lives complaining and dodging responsibility find neither happiness nor effectiveness.

SELF-ANALYSIS

To discover the kind of impact we're having on our teams, let me offer a few topics for self-analysis:

- Analyzing current relationships
- Clarifying expectations
- Living with ambiguity

- Gleaning the wisdom of new voices
- Monitoring deposits and withdrawals

ANALYZING CURRENT RELATIONSHIPS

When we examine our roles and our effectiveness, our first questions need to focus on relationships, not organizational issues or role competency. Our ability to connect with people, earn their trust, invite their opinions, and inspire them is the most important trait we bring—even more important than our experiences or skills. When we experience stress, we need to ask, "What patterns have shifted in my family, in my relationships with friends, and in my relationships with people on my team?" Quite often, significant shifts in key relationships show up as job stress. We internalize a deep sense of loss or the threat of loss, and we become defensive, demanding, or withdrawn. It's easy to see that what happens in the office affects how we relate to our spouse and children, but the reverse is also true: shifts in patterns of relationships at home can have a dramatic impact on relationships at work. Emotional health is primarily a function of relationships, not competence in our roles.

CLARIFYING EXPECTATIONS

Idealism may be a good beginning, but it seldom serves leaders and team members well as they try to form a healthy atmosphere. "Shoulds" need to be replaced by an unvarnished grasp of reality—not at the expense of hope, but with the hope-filled expectation that God will use flawed people in often messy processes to accomplish his divine purposes. People who cling to idealism inevitably become disappointed and discouraged.

LIVING WITH AMBIGUITY

All of us need to gain the skill of living in ambiguity, knowing that we live between the *already* of God's fulfilled promises and the *not yet* of those that will be fulfilled only when we see him face-to-face. High-impact leaders and team members are like a car with three gears: forward, reverse, and neutral. People with only two gears, forward and reverse, have little capacity for careful reflection. They feel uncomfortable with ambiguity and the tension of waiting. Outstanding leaders and team members, however, don't feel pressured to make instant decisions. They can listen carefully to competing interests, ask penetrating questions, invite more dialogue, and say, "I don't know" until the answer eventually surfaces. Staying in neutral for a while enables them to listen, gain more insight, reflect, involve people, and gain God's wisdom on difficult matters.

GLEANING THE WISDOM OF NEW VOICES

All of us need the challenge and the stimulation of hearing new concepts from new voices, but we need to be careful that we don't let those new voices poison our perspective. One of the marks of a healthy person and a good team member is that we're always learning, absorbing new concepts and testing new strategies. But the urge to compare is often a tragic trait of human nature. If we're not careful, we'll use the new voices as a club to condemn others who don't measure up to our new standards. With a warning against graceless comparison, we need to ask ourselves,

- Who are the new voices that have recently inspired me?

- What are some books that have challenged my thinking in the past few weeks?

- What concepts, strategies, or visions have produced in me a sense of godly discontent?

These questions focus more on *being* than *doing*, more on the ontology of who we are than on what function we perform. Too often, we focus our development strategies on roles and skills instead of heart and character, but trust is primarily a response to the internal rather than the external characteristics of a person. God created Adam and Eve as perfect human beings, but after they sinned, the curse gave them arduous tasks to do. And still today, we define ourselves and describe each other by the things we do instead of by heart and character. In the Garden, mankind shifted from acceptance, grace, and love to blame, shame, and the compulsion to prove ourselves by our performance. To recapture God's design, we need new voices that penetrate our crusty defenses and speak to our souls, not only inspiring our actions but, even more, enflaming our hearts.

MONITORING DEPOSITS AND WITHDRAWALS

There are two types of people in our lives, those who make deposits and those who make withdrawals. We can't orchestrate our lives to eliminate interactions with people who take more than they give to us, but if we are wise, we will do two crucial things: we'll limit our time with the takers, and we'll make sure we spend time with the ones who add to our emotional bank accounts. As we comprehend this principle, we'll be more understanding and patient with senior leaders. If we spent time with them each day, we'd see that 99 percent of their interactions are with people who make withdrawals. When that pastor is less than perfectly gracious in a meeting, we might conclude that he has endured too many withdrawals and too few deposits lately. An accurate perception of the effect of givers and takers in his life encourages us to be compassionate instead of judgmental.

In stagnant, discouraging, and toxic cultures, people form alliances to provide self-protection and self-validation. The people involved might claim that these interactions are important deposits in their lives, especially compared to the passivity or abuse they experience in relationships with others in the culture. But people in these alliances need to take a long, hard look at the impact of these conversations. Do they bring truth, honor, and life, or do they perpetuate resentment and gossip? In negative cultures, even "supportive" relationships make withdrawals disguised as deposits.

The commitment of each of us is to be the best team member we can be and, on our own teams, to create an inspiring culture. When we look at the culture of any organization, we don't look only at the top leaders. It is the leaders' responsibility to shape the values and the environment, but culture percolates from every nook and cranny of the organization. As we've noted earlier, a toxic environment is like carbon monoxide; you can't see it, but it'll kill you. And an inspiring culture is like perfume, filling the air with the sweet aroma of love, encouragement, passion, and a commitment to excellence.

Perhaps the most important principle in this chapter is that each person is responsible for shaping the culture. It's not acceptable to sit back and complain about how we've been mistreated or how clueless our leaders are. Remaining passive and resentful, or being demanding and furious, certainly creates a culture, but not a good one. On the spectrum of smells, we can all make the commitment to bring an aroma of life instead of carrying around the smell of cultural death.

CHAPTER 6
THE CATALYST OF CHAOS

If you have a job without aggravations, you don't have a job.
— MALCOLM FORBES

To CREATE A NEW CULTURE, you have to destroy the old one. Half measures won't do. If we try to ease our way into a new culture with as little pain as possible, we'll probably fail to make the necessary adjustments, and any change we make will be incomplete or nonexistent. Expect blood on the floor. To galvanize people's resolve to kill the old and raise up a new culture, every growing organization has to make friends with an odd ally: chaos. The commitment to change a culture is always learned from negative experiences that look like chaos but are actually open doors to a new world of creativity and growth. These experiences often take the form of failure, conflict, and power struggles, but chaos also is the result of implementing bold new plans when other people want to rest on past success. In the crucible of chaos, God forms our character, creates a new culture, and determines our destiny.

STAKES IN THE GROUND

All organizations experience change. Even churches that treasure their ancient traditions have to find ways to connect with people in a high-speed, postmodern world. Some people feel threatened by the speed of change even more than by the actual changes, and some resist change because they feel uncomfortable during the awkward time of uncertainty between the old normal and the new normal. The pace of change in our society is so fast today that leaders in every field desperately try to find ways to keep up.

In the church world, many things have changed since the Ascension, but we can count on a few constants: God's word is the source of truth, his Spirit changes lives, people value authentic leadership, and they thrive in close-knit communities of faith. These things are the stakes in the ground we can always count on. Many people who feel threatened by change are secretly (and perhaps unconsciously) wondering if their bedrock values are going to be thrown out along with the changes to worship songs, choir robes, small group content, and service times. If they are convinced that the church's core values will always be respected, they may be more willing to embrace changes in other areas.

All cultures are shifting, but thankfully, not everything in those cultures is changing, or we'd suffer from an overload of dislocation. In our family, Brenda and I still live in the same house we've enjoyed for many years, she teaches at the same school, and I do the same work with the same kind of pastors, but even in our stable world, we experience pleasant surprises, unanticipated challenges, nagging difficulties, and wonderful new opportunities. All of these demand our attention and call for us to change.

As we examine chaos as the catalyst of change, we need to remember that our people have varying capacities to embrace change. Some are terrified by it, and a few thrive in it, but they all ask a fundamental question at every step: "How does it affect me?" The way a leader navigates change may do more to define the organization's culture than any purpose statement. The path charted through threats and opportunities demonstrates the actual values of the leader, the team, and the organization. The response to chaos, then, is both a reflection of the existing culture and an open door to cultural change.

I've seen leaders experience chaos in countless ways, but three of those ways stand out as unique challenges: redefining failure, creating a sense of urgency to take advantage of opportunities, and managing conflict. Let's look at each of these.

REDEFINING FAILURE

Today, innovation is a key component of growing churches, but fresh approaches carry an inherently higher risk of failure than safer paths. Truly innovative leaders and their teams not only encourage people to dream new ideas and find new solutions but also have found a way to transform the inevitable failures into platforms for future success. They recognize the nature of risk and are realistic about the possibility—and even the probability—of failure.

What are we willing to risk for God's kingdom?

What is the point when we give up hope and quit trying to implement change?

How do we treat others when they fail?

I encourage pastors to create a culture of experimentation in which creativity is celebrated and failure isn't a tragedy. By its nature, innovation breeds a form of chaos because each day people say to themselves and each other, "I wonder if this will work." In these environments, we see versions of the "happy warrior," but here it's the "happy innovator" who is willing to risk his time, money, and reputation to see if God might bless a new way of doing things. Of course, creativity has to be guided by wisdom, but excessive caution shouldn't rule our lives. There are always far more people who say, "Don't" or "Wait" than those who eagerly say, "Let's go for it!"

Pastors and team leaders certainly don't enjoy falling on their faces, but instead of spending their emotional capital pointing fingers and defending themselves, they can develop a culture that redefines failure and replaces condemnation with tenacious hope. To create this kind of culture, leaders need to apply a few simple but important principles:

- Look in the mirror to see how you respond to failure.
- Develop a vocabulary of risk.
- Respond positively to success.
- Respond graciously to failure.

LOOK IN THE MIRROR TO SEE HOW YOU RESPOND TO FAILURE

Some of us try to be positive when others fail, but we harshly condemn ourselves for our own failures. It's very difficult to offer patience, hope, and wisdom to others when we don't experience it personally. We have to draw water from a full (or at least a filling) well.

DEVELOP A VOCABULARY OF RISK

People long to follow a leader who blends vision and wisdom, but they soon become skeptical of a wild-eyed visionary or, on the other end of the spectrum, a leader who is too cautious to take any risks at all. Think about the leaders you admire, the ones who are thoughtful, caring, and willing to attempt great things for God. How do they communicate at every level: with their top leaders, all their staff, the church, and the community? What kinds of words and phrases do they use? What are the nonverbal signals they send to those who are watching and listening? The goal isn't to take wild and crazy risks but to bring people along to trust God to accomplish his purposes—and his purposes are always big enough to enflame the hearts of his people.

RESPOND POSITIVELY TO SUCCESS

The way leaders respond to success is a predictor of how they'll respond to failure. A healthy culture celebrates success, but it always takes time to reflect on what went right and what could be better next time. And it's important to give credit where credit is due: to the Lord and to the hard work of men and women who trusted God to use them. Leaders who take too much credit for themselves erode trust, discourage followers, and drip toxins into the culture.

Success means different things to different people at different times in their lives. At one point, success for me was determined by how much money I made. Today, I measure it by how much impact God gives me in the lives of leaders. Bob Buford, the founder of Leadership Network, has written eloquently about the need to shift our attention from success to significance. I believe there is a category after that: fulfillment, the sweet spot at the intersection of God's gifting in our lives, people's needs, and our joy at seeing lives changed.

RESPOND GRACIOUSLY TO FAILURE

Many people come from families and church cultures where failure was condemned in one way or another. There may not have been name-calling and raised voices, but the one responsible got "that look" that spoke a thousand words of blame and disappointment. Attempting great things for God always results in a mixed bag of success and failure. Expect it, and don't come unglued when failure happens. Look people in the eye, reassure them with an affirmation that they went for it with boldness and faith, and make a point of asking two forward-looking questions:

1. What did you learn?

2. What will you do next time?

Ironically, some Christians feel particularly threatened by failure because they believe that God's involvement should guarantee success. They forget that responding to failure with faith is the cornerstone of the Christian life, and the examples in the scriptures are almost limitless. Failure isn't the end of the world. In fact, if we develop an optimistic, forward-thinking culture of experimentation, failure can be the platform to learn life's greatest lessons so that we can continue to think the unimaginable, dream the impossible, and attempt incredible things for God. Redefining failure for your team and your church is a vital part of creating a strong, inspiring culture. Stop playing not to lose, and start playing to win.

Every organization experiences natural cycles of growth and decline. British author Charles Handy has popularized the Sigmoid Curve to encourage leaders of change. The cycle begins with an energizing vision and moves into a growth mode. If momentum isn't sustained, energy gradually subsides, and passion erodes into empty regimentation and lifeless institutionalization. Finally, decline leads to stagnation and death. At that point, people remember the "good old days" when the vision was fresh and strong. In the diagram, point A marks the period when the vision begins to fade, but decline doesn't occur until later, at point B.

VISION, GROWTH, DECLINE, STAGNATION, AND DEATH

Churches may be at point A when a successful building campaign has been completed, a new small group emphasis has doubled the size of that ministry, a bold outreach has seen hundreds come to Christ and join the church, a new discipleship philosophy and strategy has profoundly shaped people's lives, or any other major emphasis in the church has been successful. At that moment, leaders and followers are tempted to take a deep breath and conclude, "Wow, that was great. Let's take a break for a while." They don't realize that the failure to capitalize on the momentum is the beginning point of decline. In fact, most leaders don't recognize the need for change until point B, when decline has already become a reality.

Great leaders have the foresight to predict the need at point A for a fresh vision and change, before decline sets in at point B. Communicating this perspective is a difficult task because very few people, if anyone, in the organization sees a need to "fix" what isn't broken. At this pivotal moment, visionary leaders need to infuse a successful system with a sense of urgency that change is necessary—right now before it's too late! But this attempt carries a risk. Communicating a fresh vision for change during a time of peace is seen by some as a power trip on the part of the leader. They question his motives—and perhaps his sanity. Great leaders, though, are often misunderstood, especially when they create chaos when everyone expects a time of tranquility.

If a leadership team takes action at point A and infuses the church with a new vision, strategy, and heart, they can change the shape of the curve and experience another growth cycle. The time between the envisioning of the new wave at point A and the upward movement after a period of preparation (often two or three years) is full of doubt, fear, and questions—a time of chaos.

When the leader makes the change at point A, he will inevitably incur misunderstanding from many and resistance from some. In the season of chaos between point A and point B, people are in a state of flux, routines have been disturbed, and the security of the familiar is absent. This chaos can certainly be avoided, but only if the leader waits until it's obvious the change is needed at point B. At this point, however, it's too late to stay on top of the game. We must change before the need to change is obvious. Constant growth means consistent chaos. Consequently, if an organization wants to continue to grow, the leaders must invite chaos to be their constant companion.

At every recurring point A, they recognize the need for more change, a new vision—and chaos!

If the leader and the organization are secure enough to endure it, this chaotic, flexible mode of operation will provide a path to the future. The blunt truth is that all of us experience change. The question is this: Will we change too late? When leaders understand the importance of anticipating and implementing change at point A instead of waiting until decline happens at point B, they can infuse their culture with optimism and urgency.

Urgency rarely comes from graphs on a presentation. PowerPoint slides and charts on paper may communicate important truths, but stories capture people's hearts. That's why we love novels, biographies, and movies. When I'm in a meeting and someone tells a gripping story about a danger someone courageously faced or a life God changed, people put down their PDAs, stop texting, and sit on the edge of their chairs. It takes time to find and organize a story, but it's preparation time well spent. The leader, though, doesn't have to be the only person to tell stories. In fact, it's often more powerful when team members share stories of God at work to transform individuals and families.

Strategy and a commitment to excellence are important, but they can't overcome the daunting obstacle of complacency in a leader's life. Leaders may be able to fake urgency for a while, but not for long. For it to be real and for it to last, urgency has to come from a heart gripped by people's needs and God's grace to meet those needs.

MANAGING CONFLICT

In my conversations with leaders over the decades, perhaps nothing has robbed them of joy, urgency, and vision as much or as often as enduring conflicts on their staff teams. These challenges threaten to rip the heart out of compassionate leaders, and they create an inordinate share of chaos for a leadership team. I'm convinced that many church leaders put up with far too much mediocrity and resistance among their staff members.

Most of these leaders are compassionate and don't want to upset people by correcting them or demanding compliance with spoken and unspoken norms on the team, but failure to address nagging staff problems creates a stagnant culture at best, and at worst, a toxic one. Actually, I've never consulted with a pastor who didn't need to fire at least one of his staff members. I've heard all the reasons and excuses for keeping resistant, negative people on a team, but I don't buy them. When I hear leaders protest my advice to fire someone, I tell them, "You'll pay a price either way; either a brief and relatively small price by replacing the person, or a much bigger and long-term price if you let the person continue to sour the team and do a poor job in an important ministry area at the church. It's your choice which price you'll pay."

When chaos occurs on a staff team, the first thing the leader should do is look at herself and ask some questions: "What am I doing that might be causing this difficulty?" and "What is the pattern here? Is it a long-term, pervasive issue, or an isolated event with a single individual on the team?" The leader may not have given clear directions, defined roles, or facilitated communication among team members. If the conflict or resistance is a single flare-up, the issue is usually resolved fairly easily with good listening, soothed feelings, and clear directions. But too often, conflict on a team is systemic and needs a firm hand. When leaders avoid the hard work of correction, an individual with a negative attitude can cloud the team's ability to communicate effectively and hinder creative ways to touch more people's lives. Living with mediocrity (or worse) on a staff team normalizes ineffectiveness and runs off the best people who want to serve on a team committed to excellence.

By all means, do everything you can to help struggling staff members find success and fulfillment. Conduct a performance review, be honest about the person's work and attitude, and do everything possible to create a workable, productive situation. There is a wealth of information available on managing staff, so I won't take time to articulate those principles here. There comes a point, however, when we've done all we can do to redeem a staff member, and it hasn't worked. Now it's time to help that person transition as graciously as possible. Provide assistance in helping him find a suitable placement, but don't let your team suffer and God's vision languish any longer.

In selecting outstanding staff members, look for more than positive references and experience in certain skills. Dig deeper to uncover the person's passions and commitments. When I consult with church leaders about hiring or promoting staff, I suggest they ask four questions:

1. Competence: Can you do the job?
2. Character: Can I trust you?
3. Chemistry: Can you fit in our culture?
4. Capacity: Can you grow with us?

Two crucial mistakes I've seen in the composition of church leadership teams are keeping mediocre people too long and hiring people too quickly without doing all the homework needed to make a good decision. A good rule to follow is, *make people decisions slowly.* If you rush to hire someone to fill a slot, you may spend countless hours trying to make the person fit, or working through the pain (for everyone) of replacing the person who didn't fit.

EMBRACING THE CHAOS OF CHANGE

Every team leader knows that some people on the team are more eager to jump on the train of a new idea than others, and there's always someone who drags his feet yelling, "No, it won't work!" up to the day the team celebrates the success of the venture. Leaders need to recognize that people have different degrees of capability to embrace the chaos of change. Perceptive leaders develop the ability to anticipate the response of each person to a challenge or a new opportunity.

To understand people and their responses to change, we need to remember that all of us instinctively ask, "What's in it for me?" Perceptive leaders also learn to ask themselves and their team members two other questions:

1. What about me embraces or resists this particular change?

2. What about the culture of our team embraces or resists this change?

An individual may embrace or resist change for any number of reasons: a simple preference, a core value, peer pressure, groupthink, or the need to defend staked-out turf. As I've observed people in times of change, I've noticed that the change itself is often a minor issue in a person's response. The more important factors that shape team members' responses are the way the change is presented, the level of respect for the person who presents it, the rate of change, and the clarity of the team member's role in the process of change. For instance, one team member will gladly embrace any new idea if Susan suggests it because she trusts Susan. If Bill had suggested exactly the same concept, she would have shot it down with a vengeance! Those factors give confidence (or erode it) in the crucial time when people are internalizing the new reality of a changing world.

The Diffusion of Innovations model (popularized by Everett Rogers) helps us understand the terrain of our teams and our churches as we propose change. According to this theory, people adopt one of five roles in their response to change. In my book *What's Shakin' Your Ladder?* I identify these as excited embracers, early embracers, middlers, late embracers, and never embracers. The distribution of these roles in a group forms a bell curve.

Excited embracers make up 2 percent of a population. They are the dreamers and visionaries who are usually recognized as leaders or policymakers.

Early embracers are 18 percent of a group. They are respected and influential, and they eagerly get on board when the concept is explained. Leaders treasure these people on their teams.

Middlers are the largest part of the population, about 60 percent of people in the group. They feel more comfortable with the status quo, and they listen very carefully to anyone who resists change. They are willing to get on board only when they are convinced that everybody else will, too.

Late embracers make up 18 percent of the people in a large group. They resist change as long as possible, offering objections all along the way. Eventually, they will go along with the majority, but with a large measure of skepticism and without any enthusiasm at all.

Never embracers are 2 percent of the group. They are steadfastly committed to the past, and they continue to resist change long after the rest of the team is working hard to achieve success.

If you can convince the majority of middlers to support the initiative, you are on your way.

In most cases, the battle is to win the middlers. You won't need to work hard to convince excited embracers and early embracers of the value of your new idea. Late embracers won't be convinced until the idea becomes reality, and the never embracers are a lost cause. But if you can convince the majority of middlers to support the initiative, you are on your way.

Most middlers prefer the known to the unknown, the present's certainty to the future's uncertainty. This doesn't mean that middlers are closed to reason or can't catch the excitement of a new vision, but they tend to support the status quo unless they are given a good reason to change. They need to be assured that change won't result in loss of quality and won't cause them to lose their important role on the team.

Make early embracers your allies. Usually they are respected members of the team and the church, so their opinions are given serious consideration, and their leadership is usually followed. Make a list of the early embracers and solicit their active support. Ask them to endorse the new proposal in formal meetings and informal discussions, and enlist their help with the middlers. Explain that hallway and parking lot conversations often influence middlers more than anything else, and let them know that in every meeting, they will make the difference between failure and success. Church leaders don't have any choice about the range of people who attend the church and show up at business meetings. Invariably, late embracers drag their feet and never embracers object to anything and everything. But leaders certainly have the authority and responsibility to select staff members and top volunteers. Careful selection is not an option but a necessity—it makes all the difference in how the team functions, as well as in how (or even if) God's purposes are fulfilled. Look for patterns in people's responses to the chaos of failure or the chaos created by a fresh vision. Some are resistant to only one or two items on the agenda, but others display a pervasive pattern of negativity.

Let me be clear: *know your people.* Give chronically resistant people every opportunity to change, but if they don't change their attitudes in a reasonable amount of time (you'll know), you can't afford to have an anchor on the team holding you back.

I don't subscribe to the "convoy theory" that a team moves only as fast as the slowest person. Good leaders have the ability to pull people along more quickly than they would normally move.

But leaders shouldn't have anyone on a team who is slower and more resistant than a middler. Of course, we certainly respect people who ask penetrating questions. That's incredibly valuable to a team! But we need people who ask those questions with an eye toward solutions and a commitment to take bold action when the team has charted a course. Don't settle for anything less.

In times of chaos, leaders need to be observant about the types of responses they can expect from team members, and they need to marshal their primary resources in the organization—the early embracers—to help get others on board with the new plan. Change may be thrust upon the team or the church by outside forces, such as a downturn in the economy or demographic shifts in the community, or high-impact leaders may infuse change into the system by anticipating an opportunity for growth at point A. The leader's response to the chaos of change reflects the current culture, but more important, the experience of chaos offers a perfect classroom to impart a new culture to the team and the body of believers. No matter how well a leader anticipates change and communicates with others, resistance is inevitable. Author and humorist Robert Orben quipped, "Sometimes I get the feeling that the whole world is against me, but deep down I know that's not true. Some of the smaller countries are neutral."

The Value of Honest Feedback

In an open culture that values experimentation and learning, we treasure people who help us reflect more deeply. That's the role Benson Karanja played in my life when I was president of Beulah Heights University. Benson trusted me enough to challenge my thinking, disagree with me, and help me think more clearly than ever before. He was always willing to ask hard questions, often questions no one else was willing to ask out loud, but he didn't ask difficult questions because he wanted to throw up roadblocks. He asked so we could find the very best solutions to the challenges we faced. In our relationship, disagreement wasn't a threat. It only created a context for us to explore and experiment together. All leaders need someone like Benson who is ruthlessly honest, thoroughly good-hearted, willing to patiently probe the depths of an issue, eager to pursue workable solutions, and supportive of the team at every point in the process. I wouldn't be doing what I'm doing today if it weren't for Benson. He is a great gift to me.

People don't bring the same level of insight, skill, and passion to every subject. Some may be passionate about children's ministry, but they couldn't care less about music. In meetings, I've learned to discover what each person brings to the table so that I can appropriately value her for her area of expertise and enthusiasm. In a similar way, some people on the team have more relational and emotional authenticity than others. When perceptive, caring people speak about others' emotional responses to a service or a program, I listen intently to what they have to say. But if the topic of conversation is the budget, I pay close attention to the accountant who has a clear grasp of the numbers, even if he's not relationally perceptive. Good leaders are observant. They notice what makes people tick, the resources they bring to each issue, and their level of integrity.

Chaos—no matter what the cause might be—is a test that shows what people and organizations are really made of. Experiencing times of chaos is like squeezing a sponge: whatever was lurking there before comes out. But seasons of chaos are only tragic if leaders fail to take advantage of them. If we respond with insight, courage, and hope, they become catalysts for incredible growth—for the church and for each person on the team.

CHAPTER 7
CHANGING VEHICLES

Reinvent yourself every three years . . . so that you can remain relevant and able to make new contributions in a world of constant change. . . . Reinvention is the key to longevity.
— STEPHEN R. COVEY

WE'VE SEEN THAT CHANGING THE culture of a team or a church doesn't happen by magic, and it doesn't happen quickly. It's relatively easy to change a program, but it's more difficult to change the ministry philosophy and strategy that shapes the implementation of a program. But these are relatively easy compared to changing the culture, because culture reflects our most sacred values of integrity, trust, and heart, as well as how we implement our values in every relationship and program. Changing a culture requires clear thinking, concerted effort, enormous courage, and tenacious consistency. But first, we need to recognize what needs to change.

VISION AND VEHICLE

If I wanted to travel to London from my home in Atlanta, it wouldn't matter if I had a Lamborghini or a Rolls Royce—a car wouldn't get me to Piccadilly. A car could get me to the airport or to a port where I could get on a ship, but a car simply isn't designed to travel across the ocean. No amount of wishing or claiming promises will make the car a suitable vehicle to reach the destination I desire. Now there's absolutely nothing wrong with a car to get me to anywhere on the contiguous land mass. It's perfect for that purpose, but not for ocean travel. If London is my vision, I have to abandon the vehicle I'm using and find another to get me there.

This analogy fits the situation for many church leaders. We may have a very good vehicle (our organizational structure and personnel) to achieve a limited vision, but the one we are currently using may not be able to take us to the place God wants us to go. Like the traveler, no amount of wishing or tinkering with the engine will solve the problem. We can try to put wings on a car, but it still won't fly. We can attach a sail or a rudder to the car, but it won't make the ocean voyage. We need a new vehicle, often a radically new one, if we're going to achieve all that God has for our team and our church. This doesn't make the current vehicle "bad." There's a difference between *bad* and *wrong*. The vehicle we've been using isn't morally deficient or evil in any way. It simply can't produce the results we need. It's the wrong vehicle to take us where we want to go.

When I talk to pastors and explain this principle, they almost always instantly get it. The lights come on in their eyes, and they suddenly realize that they've been trying to drive a car to London! No wonder they've experienced so much frustration. After a few minutes, I often ask, "Now that you see that the vehicle of your organization can't get you to the destination of your vision, which one needs to change—the vehicle or the destination?" This may seem like a simplistic, rhetorical question, but actually, it's crucial. When leaders keep butting their heads against a wall day after day—or, using our metaphor, they keep driving up to the beach on the East Coast and realizing they can't go any farther toward London—many of them scale back their vision to match the capabilities of their organizational vehicle. That's precisely the wrong solution! When they finally realize how their existing structure and personnel aren't capable of achieving their vision, their frustration melts into a firm conviction to do the only reasonable thing: change the vehicle.

When I meet with pastors and discuss the principle of creating an organizational vehicle to fulfill their vision, I want to find out if their vision is clear and strong, and I want to help them see if their organizational structure and people can take them to reach that vision. Dr. Gerald Brooks (www.growingothers.com) has helped me think through this issue by using a series of test questions.

1. The heart test: Is the vision burning brightly in the heart of the leader, both in public descriptions of where God is leading him and passionately in his heart?

2. The leadership test: Do the top leaders in the church share this vision, or are they apathetic or resistant? Are these the people who can take the church to the vision's destination?

3. The organization test: How well does the current organizational structure work to achieve the vision? What are the bottlenecks? Which aspects are cars that can't take you there? Which ones are planes or ships?

4. The recruiting test: Are new hires and volunteers on board with the vision, or are they still a work in progress?

5. The message test: Is the vocabulary of the vision consistent and strong in every part of the church? Is the message of the vision reflected in sermons, written materials, the budget, signs, and conversations about the priorities of the church?

6. The planning test: Is the church's vision your staff's benchmark for strategic planning in every area?

7. The facility test: Do facilities, including their layout, design, and decor, reflect the vision?

8. The money test: Does the budget demonstrate the vision's priorities?

9. The pragmatism test: Does the vision make sense? Is it both God-sized and workable? Can you see it happening? Is it so global that it doesn't capture anyone's heart, or is it appropriately targeted?

10. The capacity test: How well does the capacity of the current organizational structure and personnel match the vision?

11. The clarity test: Can people throughout the organization articulate the vision clearly and with passion? If you ask people who come out the door after the service on Sunday morning to articulate the vision of the church, could they share it clearly and with enthusiasm?

12. The counsel test: Who are the outside voices that are helping to shape the vision and the vehicle to fulfill it?

13. The growth test: How do the ministries of the church need to be organized to capitalize on the next two stages of growth?

How do we know if a vision is from God? One of the measures is that it has to be something so big that it requires God's wisdom and power to pull it off. Anything less is just a good idea. God's vision is to redeem not only individuals but the entire creation. He's not just making new men and women; he's going to re-create the entire universe in the New Heaven and New Earth. That's a big vision! Small visions don't enflame people's hearts—yours or those who follow you. Don't dumb down your vision to instinctively understand the power of a big, compelling vision. When he was an old man, English sculptor Henry

Moore was asked, "Now that you are 80, you must know the secret of life. What is it?"

Moore smiled and answered, "The secret of life is to have a task, something you do your entire life, something you bring everything to, every minute of the day for your whole life. And the most important thing is: It must be something you cannot possibly do."[1] That's a good benchmark for our visions, too.

Some churches are rocking along pretty well. They have a bold, clear vision, and they enjoy a culture of creativity and experimentation, so their people are conditioned to embrace new ideas. Many churches, though, have been doing the same things so long that they don't even know other vehicles exist. To change the metaphor, these leaders need to heal the infection before they can perform a heart transplant. If they attempt surgery before they've dealt with the infection, the patient— their team and their church—will suffer and die. The first step for them is to get the body as healthy as possible, and then take bold steps to change the culture.

CLARITY, CONGRUENCE, AND COURAGE

When I take my wife to a lovely restaurant, we enjoy the nice tablecloth, flowers, soft music, gentle lighting, courteous service, and wonderful meal. But a few inches beyond that idyllic setting is a very different environment: the kitchen. That's where people are running around cooking, preparing plates, and fussing with each other so that they can provide the perfect dinner for my wife and me. In the same way, when people come to a church's worship service, they enjoy the best and the most beautiful setting we can provide. Sometimes they say to each other, "Wow, I'd love to work in a place like this. It's wonderful!" But they have no idea that the real work of the church is much more like the kitchen, and they are shocked to find that making a delicious entree is a messy process. Leading a church isn't much different from being a chef in a busy, chaotic kitchen.

Quite often, ministry leaders and board members have offered ideas, suggestions, and plans that sounded great, but may not have been in alignment with the original vision. The leader didn't want to discourage the creativity of those people, so he smiled and went along. "It can't hurt anything, can it?" he wondered. But eventually the leader wakes up and realizes that too many compromises have been made and that the organization's vision is significantly different from his own. To remedy the conflict, too many leaders conclude that it's easier to adjust their own sense of God's calling and vision than to expend all the energy it would require to bring the entire leadership team, plans, and programs back into alignment with the original vision.

Maybe he's tired. Maybe he's discouraged. Maybe he's tired of fighting and feeling alone, and maybe he realizes all too well that it will be a colossal struggle to turn the team around. But if he continues to give in and support a vision he doesn't really believe in, he's not being true to himself, to God, or to his people. The leader has subordinated his God-given vision to a group of people who are taking the church to a different place. The conflict probably isn't between good and evil. Their vision and their destination are probably noble and worthy, too, but the pastor has to own a vision, not acquiesce to someone else's. We're not talking about a dictatorship or a heavy-handed style. We're talking about the importance—the necessity—of visionary leadership. The members of the team must be in line with the leader's vision and core values. If they aren't, he can't lead them. A pastor can't chart a course, plan effectively, and motivate his troops if his people aren't on board with his vision and core values.

Organizational congruence is necessary if staff members are going to achieve God's vision and work effectively as a team. Without it, there's only confusion and conflict.

When a leader's vision and values are aligned with the organization's goals and the hearts of the team members, the congruence will be reflected in everything they do. For example, a local Atlanta church states that one of its core values is missions. This value is demonstrated in planning, budgeting, personnel, and even in prayer. The budget shows a large percentage of the church's income going to mission projects, and the missions department has more staff members and volunteers than any other department in the church. A glance at the church calendar shows that it's peppered with missions-related activities. Missionaries, mission trips, and mission funding and prayer are high priorities on the pastor's schedule, too. This focus demonstrates organizational congruence at the church around a compelling vision.

As I've worked with church leaders, I've observed them moving through the following phases as they've implemented new strategies, especially in changing their cultures:

1. Entrepreneurial, or the *discovery* phase, when the strategy is seen as viable: it can be done!

2. Emerging, or the *growth* phase, when credibility is crucial: the leader can be trusted.

3. Established, or the *maintenance* phase, when stability is achieved: the systems are in place and functioning well.

4. Eroding, or the *survival* phase, when the church is vulnerable: signs of decline are obvious.

5. Enterprising, or the *reinvention* phase, when leaders adapt to a fresh vision and new strategies: they adjust so they can grow again.

The only way to avoid eroding is to keep going back to being entrepreneurial. When leaders rest on their past successes, they become organizationally flabby—soft and passive. In fact, the more successful an organization has been in the past, the more likely it is to fail in the future. Without the constant infusion of entrepreneurial spirit, flourishing can lead to floundering!

Churches must "re-dream" the dream or discover a new compelling vision for their existence. For a leadership team and those they lead to continue developing and growing, they must focus on the organizing principles of the stages ahead. Leadership styles and the key issues to be addressed are different for each stage of the cycle. Effective leaders understand the cycle and are able to adapt their leadership to the corresponding needs of each stage.

The danger is that the old mental models will remain in place and that the desire for the security and familiarity of the past will win out over the opportunity of the moment to embrace and live out a new dream. Your thoughts will create your attitude, which leads to action. The Chinese characters that form the word *crisis* are a combination of *danger* and *opportunity*. Every crisis calls us to face danger, but we need to redefine it as opportunity. Olan Hendrix, author of *Three Dimensions of Leadership*, observed, "Generally, religious organizations start out with a goal orientation . . . deteriorate to a task orientation . . . and finally degenerate to a bottom-line control organization." Don't let that happen to you!

Your effectiveness will always depend on your ability to see the future. To be an effective leader, you must understand the difference between *change* and *transition*. *Change* is the event (for example, the first vision is realized, the founding pastor is gone, the community demographics have changed), and *transition* is the emotional, psychological, and social response to that change. In most situations, not enough attention is paid to the transition side, and leaders often move forward without realizing that the congregation, staff, or both are not processing the change at the same level they are.

Your future can be bright if:

- You have a compelling vision.

- You have aligned the resources and ministries of the church to the vision.

- You understand the process of change and transition.
- You have the blessing of the Lord.

Strategic planning needs to be written in pencil because in a dynamic, changing environment, strategic planning needs constant evaluation and adjustment.

Congruence is a key component of an effective organizational vehicle. It is clear focus that organizes people, plans, and funding, and it flows from the church's vision, mission, and core values, permeating every department of the church. Of course, some churches do a better job than others, but the fact is, most leadership teams never even consider the importance of congruence. They just think, talk, and plan the way they've always done. The results are pockets of wonderful success, with some department leaders competing with others for resources, and some apathetic about what happens in other parts of the church. The absence of congruence is like a plane with one wing missing, a ship without a rudder, or a car with a flat tire. The organization can't fulfill a God-sized vision, even in its local market, without the alignment of people, plans, and funding around a common purpose.

CONGRUENCE AND STRATEGIC PLANNING

An old adage says that the devil is in the details, but actually, I believe that the fulfillment of a vision is in the details. Global statements have a place, but they need to be backed up with specific, strategic plans to fulfill the vision. Developing a healthy culture is the "soft side" of leadership, but strategic planning, the "hard side" of leadership, is also essential. The two complement each other. When staff members and church attenders hear concrete plans designed to accomplish the church's purpose, they trust their leaders, and the culture takes a step forward. If, however, they always hear glowing vision statements without seeing how the vision is going to be realized, they become skeptical of their leaders. Stagnant, discouraging, and toxic cultures usually aren't short on vision.

In fact, their leaders often communicate grand and glorious pictures of the future. Many of these cultures are unhealthy because their leaders don't back up their lofty words with specific plans. Their people soon learn that they are full of hot air.

Strategic planning enables a team and every department in the church to work together for a common goal. It's the hallmark of congruence, and it's essential to healthy church cultures. Strategic planning is an acquired skill. When a team learns the principles of strategic planning and gains some experience, it becomes second nature for them to value the congruence of vision, people, and resources. A healthy, powerful culture moves a team and a church body toward the ultimate objectives God has given them.

I've noticed that many leaders don't have a framework for decision making. They just do whatever looks best at the moment. Perhaps the simplest and clearest template for planning is to follow the acronym SMART. Plans need to be *s*pecific, *m*easurable, *a*ccountable, *r*easonable, and *t*imely.

When presented with a complicated decision that could change the direction of the organization and shape the culture, we need to ask four questions; and it is important that we ask them in this order.

1. Is the program in line with our vision, mission, and core values? No matter how great an idea or opportunity, if the program isn't in line with the vision, we must say no to it. Most church leaders use their vision statements to say yes, but they rarely use it to say no and eliminate options. If everything imaginable fits under the umbrella of the vision, perhaps the vision statement is too broad and needs to be refined and clarified.

2. Do we have the organizational and human capacity—and the heart—to do this? The program may be so large that it creates enormous stress for the entire team, or perhaps we don't have the right people on the team to accomplish the objective, our facilities and volunteer manpower are not be adequate to achieve the goals, or it's just not the right time.

3. *How will God be glorified?* Most leaders will ask, "Will God be glorified?" and the answer is almost always yes. When the answer is always yes, we are probably asking the wrong question. Instead, ask, "How?" This question will help us understand the true impact the decision will have on God's kingdom.

4. *How much will it cost?* This must be the last question asked. Understand the true nature of this question, and then consider it carefully. It's not "Can we afford it?" Most churches and nonprofit organizations don't have piles of money sitting around waiting to be used. The initial answer to the question of affordability is usually no. But the answer to "How much will it cost?" is different. The cost includes not only dollars but also people, resources, time, and energy pulled from other projects and programs. Most churches didn't come this far in their history because they had plenty of resources, but because their leaders were resourceful. It's not about resources; it's about being resourceful. A program that is immediately blocked by the question "Can we afford it?" might get a different response after asking all four questions. If the vision is big enough, if the people have a heart for doing it, if God will be glorified in a specific way, then the money will come.

Answering these specific questions *in this order* helps us grasp the nature of the opportunity in front of us. Then we can make principled decisions based on a larger organizational context, not on a situation, such as the amount of cash in the bank account. Using these four questions to train leaders and teams in decision making has proven to be tremendously helpful.

PASSENGERS IN THE VEHICLE

When things aren't working, leaders often prefer to change the structure of an organization because it is the easiest area to tackle. Moving boxes around on an organizational chart, reassigning who reports to whom, and handing out new titles don't rock many boats. Restructuring is a clean process, and it seems to offer the biggest gain at the least cost. In most organizations, however, reorganizing the structure doesn't make people work better or harder. This reminds me of the man who needs to clean out his garage but decides to organize his bedroom closet because it's easier. He may get finished more quickly and he may not get as dirty, but he won't have a clean garage.

Changing the organizational structure doesn't change an individual's motivation, behavior, values, or way of relating to others. Changing the culture—the way people relate to each other and their commitments—or changing the people are the only ways to see real progress. To change things in an organization, it's far more important to make adjustments to the informal connections, not the formal structure. These informal processes are the ways people communicate, make decisions, and support or hinder each other. These are far harder to identify and address than moving a box on an organizational chart, but they promise far greater rewards. We need to set the standard very high for our staff members. The stakes are far too high for us to settle for less. God has called us to partner with him to redeem the world, and like Jesus, we are willing to work with anyone who responds. As we consider our leadership teams, however, we need to continually raise the bar. Staff members who can't or won't become part of a supportive, reflective, visionary culture shouldn't be allowed to poison it.

Changing from one vehicle to another always creates chaos for a team. It's inevitable. The patterns of roles, expectations, reporting, and lines of communication that have been so familiar are now analyzed, and many are changed. Sometimes pastors realize they need to change vehicles at the moment when their church experiences a huge growth spurt. I consulted with a pastor who moved his church from a three-thousand-seat auditorium to one that holds over seven thousand. In the months leading up to the move, he assured me that he had prepared his staff and everything was under control. A month after the move, he told me, "The moment we moved into the new building, 80 percent of my staff proved to be inadequate for their new roles. We simply hadn't prepared them. We've had to scramble to equip them for the new expectations. Some are going to do fine, but a few aren't going to make the change. I thought I could just put new tires on the old vehicle and we'd reach our vision's destination that way, but now I realize that I was thinking way too small." Over the next few months, this pastor led his team in demolishing the old vehicle and creating one that promised to take them where God was leading them.

STEPS OF TRANSITION

People often say they "are afraid of" change or they "don't like" change, but in my observation, most people are far more afraid of the process of the transition from one team to another, one plan to another, or one leader to another than they are afraid of the actual change itself. Many leaders focus on changing the external in their church world, but changing a culture rivets our attention on the deeper internal issues: relationships, values, and other matters of the heart. To be a good pastor or team leader, it isn't enough only to think through what you're going to do. You must also take time to consider all of the contingencies and write a comprehensive transitional plan.

New plans always have a ripple effect in altering priorities, schedules, budgets, and, perhaps, reporting relationships in several levels of the organization. Even if only the children's ministry is directly affected by major transitions in the new strategy, the people in every other component of the church's life need to understand how the change will affect them. To minimize surprises, the team, and especially the team most involved with the changes, needs to anticipate these ripples and consider possible contingencies. If the new plan isn't carefully thought through, people in the organization may be confused and wonder about the credibility of the decision makers. Credibility is a people problem, but it's not the only relational problem to consider during a transition. The main question is, How does a leader position each team member for success?

After thinking about this question, the leader can create a written plan and then make decisions based on the plan. For example, she can ask herself these questions:

How will I approach each person?

How will I communicate the details of changes in priorities, budget, schedule, and reporting to this individual?

What information will that person need to understand this change?

You can be sure that different people will have very different perceptions of every new direction, and even if you explain things very carefully, some of them will disagree. That's especially true when you need to remove someone from a high-profile position.

William Bridges, a noted expert on change and transition, explains in his most recent book, *Managing Transitions: Making the Most of Change*, that the reason change agents fail is that they focus on the solution instead of the problem. This may seem counterintuitive to forward-thinking, visionary leaders, but Bridges teaches that people need to be gripped by the need before they will embrace the solution. In fact, he believes that 90 percent of a leader's efforts should be spent on selling the problem and helping people understand what is *not* working. He rightly claims that people don't perceive the need for a solution if they don't fully grasp the problem.

I've listened to countless pastors explain their vision to me, to a group of pastors, or to their congregations. Most of them focus their attention on the benefits they will enjoy when God fulfills a particular objective in their church and community.

Comparatively few of them take time to paint the picture of people's needs so that hearts are stirred. When people are touched by pain, heartache, and lostness in others' lives, they'll eagerly embrace solutions to meet those needs. That's the power of organizations like World Vision and Compassion International. They don't just ask people for money for kids. Before they mention money, they show the faces of children who live in poverty and ignorance, and only then do they show how a person's contribution can effectively change a child's life. Is this manipulative? Not in the least. It's simply the most effective way to move the hearts of people so that they want to participate in meeting the needs of hurting people.

Good planning is essential in creating a positive culture, and it works at all times with all people. The responsibility for a successful transition is in the hands of the leader making the change. Assimilating people into leadership roles is one of the most difficult challenges we face. However, if we properly prepare and execute a transition plan, and if we take responsibility for the changes we institute, we'll build trust, provide clear direction, and reinforce a positive culture.

TRANSITIONS IN A TEAM'S CULTURE

Some of us look at the size of our church and conclude that it's impossible to make any difference in its culture. The vehicle of organizational structure and personnel is, we're convinced, what it is, and it will always be the same. We've been to conferences, prayed, and talked to other leaders until our tongues hang out, but nothing has changed. Before we give up completely and fade into passive resentment of leaders or followers (depending on our position), we need to understand that our role in implementing change should be focused only on those immediately around us. We don't need to fret about everybody, but we can take bold steps to make a difference in the culture of our own teams. In an article in *Leader to Leader*, Dave Logan, John King, and Halee Fisher-Wright identify smaller clusters of people they call "tribes." A small organization may have only one tribe, but large churches and other corporate entities might contain hundreds or even thousands of tribes. The authors observe that changing a tribe's culture from toxic to inspiring follows five distinct stages. Change doesn't happen by trying to jump two or three stages at once, but instead by slowly and carefully building trust and authenticity to move up one stage at a time. Using the language of our scale of five types of culture, the authors report:[3]

- About 2 percent of tribes are toxic. They create and perpetuate a poisonous environment like a street gang. Life, they are convinced, is totally unfair, and each person is left to dominate or to defend himself at all costs.

- Following a bell curve, 25 percent of tribes are discouraging. People perceive themselves as hopeless victims who have no power (and no responsibility) to change the atmosphere.

- Approximately half of all organizations are composed of stagnant tribes. Here, effort is expended on achieving personal success, personal advancement, and personal gain. In these tribes, people are divided into the "haves" who are beating the system and the "have-nots" who aren't making the progress they desire. The words "I," "me," and "my" dominate conversations.

- Accepting tribes are found in 22 percent of organizations. In these productive and supportive environments, shared values and teamwork focus attention on the common goals of the group.

- Only 2 percent of tribal cultures inspire people to devote their shared energies to creative solutions aimed at achieving the seemingly impossible. This kind of culture is rare, and it is also quite vulnerable to slipping back to a state of reduced creativity, confused values, and selfish ambitions.

Senior pastors can work hard to take all the tribes in their churches on a journey from where they are to become inspiring communities, but the first step is to work on their own leadership team. And the rest of the staff members need to realize that they can't change the whole culture of the organization, but can take their own teams on a journey from one stage to the next. There is no magic bullet to transform a team into an inspiring culture overnight. Those who try to make that happen frustrate themselves and disappoint their teams. To see change in a team's culture, the first step is to take a good, hard look at our own perceptions, attitudes, and behaviors. Change begins with us.

Healthy cultures thrive because the right people are in the right roles sharing a common vision and working with congruent plans, priorities, and resources. All these elements are essential. As we've seen, too many leaders put up with less than healthy cultures because they aren't willing to pay the price to destroy the old and create the new. Changing an unhealthy culture to a strong, vibrant one requires both a sledgehammer and a potter's wheel. We have to be ruthless to attack systems (not people) that block us from achieving our new objectives, but we also need to carefully mold a new culture with gentleness, wisdom, and strength—like a skilled potter making a beautiful vase.

Good leaders ruthlessly wield sledgehammers to destroy inadequate organizational vehicles, but they pull out a wider range of tools to use with people. Team members are closely tied to the old structures, so it's wise to use the right tool to communicate effectively with each staff member. I've known some who needed only a light tap to shatter old thinking and get them into the new vehicle, but I've also had to use a twenty-pound sledgehammer to make a dent with a few people. My goal in all cases isn't to hurt them, but to help them make the transition from the old to the new. And all along, I've painted pictures as clearly as possible to show them what we're missing, capture their hearts by showing them the needs of people, and show how they play a crucial role in the new vehicle. Communicating clearly and powerfully is my responsibility. I explain that each of us "has to give up a little to go up a lot." If I've observed them very well, I can anticipate how each one will respond, and I know how big a tap I need to make to help that individual let go of the old way of doing things and take steps toward a new, stronger, more effective vehicle.

One of the most interesting questions to ask leaders is, Who are the real power brokers in your meetings? At first, most of them will say, "Well, I am." They have the title and the role, but quite often, the informal power is owned by a sour person who fills the room with doubts, or a person who sees every decision through the grid of money instead of God's calling, or someone who demands that everyone agree with him on any subject. When these people (and these are just a few examples) are given informal power in a meeting, moving forward is as hard as pushing a rope uphill. This kind of culture has to be crushed so that a positive one can be created.

In these times of transition, people often become territorial—precisely at the time we want them to be more open to working as a team. In a meeting, for example, if a ministry leader insists on clinging to a room assignment because that's where and when one of her groups has met for years, but I've asked her to make an adjustment, I first go to that person privately and say something like this: "Beth, I know that group is important to you and it's inconvenient to ask them to meet at another time, but I need you to help me think and plan for the whole church, not just for your department. Can you do that for me?" Usually, that's enough, just a light tap, and she gets on board. But if she still resists my direction in the next meeting, I turn to her with a heavier hammer and say, "Beth, I've noticed that every time we have conversations about making the transitions we've been discussing, you want to protect your department from any changes. Your department is very important to all of us, but we are all making some tradeoffs to make this work. I need for you to work with the rest of us. We've talked about this privately. Resistance to change bogs us down and takes our attention away from where we need to go. Can I count on you from this point forward?" Then I turn to the rest of the group and say, "Now, where were we?" And we continue our meeting.

When leaders face transitions like those described in this chapter, they often instinctively ask, "How much am I going to bleed when I go through this?" But that's the wrong question. A better question is, "I know I'm going to bleed. How can I help my team get healthy as quickly as possible?" When a surgeon has to amputate a man's leg, does the man want her to use a scalpel or a butter knife? If she uses the butter knife, she'll eventually get the leg off, but the process will be very messy. The biggest risk for a patient with a diseased leg is to avoid surgery, and if you wait until you're 100 percent sure that surgery is necessary, it's probably too late and the patient will die. If surgery is needed, the patient will do best if a skilled surgeon uses the sharpest scalpel she can find. That's the way to get the operation over as quickly as possible and protect the health of the patient. If you have to fire three people on your team, you and the rest of your team will bleed far more if you fire them one at a time over several months.

In healthy cultures where skilled, caring leaders communicate often and well with their teams and value their input, risks are minimized because people feel affirmed, have clear roles and goals, and don't become embroiled in turf wars. action carries the risk of increasing levels of misunderstanding and distrust.

Don't put up with a deficient vehicle any longer. Destroy what you need to destroy, and create something beautiful in its place. The sledgehammer, though, has to be used with precision. Destroy possessive turf wars on your team; take the hammer to decisions that are based solely on money instead of vision; hit the spirit of blaming others and being exclusive; and obliterate the spirit of secret alliances, suspicion, and distrust. The free CULTURE survey (www.freeculturesurvey.com) will surface elements that need attention in your environment. When you see them, take a deep breath, think carefully, and pray deeply, then pick up your sledgehammer and begin destroying any unhealthy segments as you create a new culture for your team and your church.

CHAPTER 8
YES, YOU CAN!

I've missed more than 9000 shots in my career. I've lost almost 300 games. Twenty-six times I've been trusted to take the winning shot and missed. I've failed over and over again in my life. And that is why I succeed. —MICHAEL JORDAN

IS IT POSSIBLE TO TRANSFORM a culture? Some of us think that it seems almost too good to be true. But yes, it's not only possible but also the most productive work we can do because it has a dramatic, multiplied impact—on the team, in the church, and throughout the community. To take a team through the labyrinth of changing the culture, we need to engage their hearts and minds. Gifted teachers know that asking a great question is often more valuable than an hour of brilliant lecture. Questions challenge a person's thinking and draw her into the process of exploring solutions.

Gifted teachers know that asking a great question is often more valuable than an hour of brilliant lecture.

The best ones are open questions that don't have simple, quick answers. They ask why and how, not just what and who. Sometimes, though, a simple question (and its answer) provides the foundation for a richer, deeper, more thought-provoking open question that follows it.

First, ask poignant questions to yourself. I'd suggest the following:

PERSONAL REFLECTION

- Who am I? Where does my identity come from?
- What matters most to me?
- How well does my daily schedule relate to what matters most to me?
- Beyond roles and paychecks, what is my deepest, most compelling motivation? Really?
- How do I define success?
- Where am I in the process of learning, growing, and changing as a person and as a leader?

Don't rush your answers. Carve out some time alone, away from the hectic pace of the office, so you can genuinely ponder these things. Ask God to give insight into your heart, your desires, and your values—and listen to his Spirit as you think and pray. Leaders report that some answers come easily, but when they are committed to being ruthlessly honest with God, some questions challenge them to the core. Don't feel that you have to have all the answers tied up with a nice bow. Give yourself room to keep thinking, praying, and reflecting on your deepest motivations.

In a series of conversations with your team, ask them some penetrating questions. Listen carefully to their answers without correcting them or defending your positions. You'll know you're really listening if, when someone says something you don't agree with, you reply, "That's a very interesting point. Tell me more." I suggest you ask these questions:

QUESTIONS ABOUT THE TEAM'S PERCEPTION OF THE LEADER

- What are three things you'd like to change about our team?
- What are three things you want to be sure we don't change?
- What do you want me to do for you?
- What are you afraid I'm going to do?
- What helps you serve with a full heart? What hinders or clouds your motivation?
- Is there anything lingering in your mind or on your heart that you want to talk about? Nothing is off-limits; anything goes.

These questions are open enough to encompass the full range of challenges, relationships, systems, and motivations on a team. In fact, if the conversation doesn't go deeper than the level of job descriptions, it hasn't touched people's hearts.

Many pastors and teams also invite input about the culture from a wider range of midlevel leaders. They may ask each ministry director to schedule times to involve her staff and top volunteers, or the pastor may want to hold a town hall meeting.

Large meetings are expedient, but they aren't conducive to the kinds of interactions needed to talk openly about the culture of the ministry team. I'd recommend that the ministry leaders follow the example of the pastor and lead their teams in open dialogue about the things that matter to them. The following are some questions for these teams:

- In what ways does our operating system (delegation, meetings, reporting, follow up, and so on) provide a forum for honest dialogue among team members and the ministry leader? How does the system hinder this kind of dialogue?

- Do we have the tools and resources we need to fulfill God's vision for our team? If not, what do we need?

- How well do we cultivate a culture of experimentation that celebrates taking risks to accomplish great things for God?

- How well are we identifying, selecting, and developing rising leaders in our pipeline?

Leading a team through the chaos of culture change is challenging work, but don't let the left hand of dread and the right hand of fear squeeze hope from the hearts of your team. Invite open dialogue, but always communicate that you and the team will trust God together to find solutions. Leaders rise to meet challenges, and as Napoleon remarked, "Leaders are dealers in hope."

Don't let your team get stuck in the past. Invite team members to be honest in their assessment and creative in finding answers. In all these discussions, teams have four needs (much like a family that is going through a significant change). These are:

1. The need for clarity
2. The need for the leader to model steady emotions, avoiding extreme highs and lows
3. The need to take action after decisions are made and the new direction is set
4. The need for security in unsettling times

In holding all these important discussions, realize that leaders are abstract communicators, but most team members think more concretely. Abstract communicators can add concrete points and illustrations to make sure they connect with people, but the vast majority of concrete thinkers have difficulty internalizing abstract thoughts. Those concepts bore them; they want specifics. Pastors need to understand that the vast majority of people on their teams and in their churches don't separate vision from strategy, which includes specific plans, meetings, roles, and schedules. It's a mistake for abstract-thinking pastors to share their vision one week and their strategy the next. They'll lose people that way. When pastors realize that their people's minds are quickset concrete, they'll make sure to simultaneously share specific plans and details of their global vision.

The leader's example of honesty and faith sets the tone for the team's future. If everyone feels like an integral part, everyone will contribute their best. Honesty invites long-buried emotions to come to the surface, so conflict is inevitable. Don't be surprised, but don't let conflict cloud the team's future. Welcome honest dialogue and seek resolution for each issue. Keep pointing people to God, his provision for the future, and his purpose for the team and the church. The way your team learns to relate to each other sets the tone for the culture of the church.

CHANGE WITH GRACE

All change is a critique of the past. If we're not careful, we can step on the toes of those we're trying to lead as we destroy the old vehicle and create a new one. Leaders need to understand what's at stake in the hearts of those who treasure the past. They may not be thrilled to change vehicles! We can't improve anything without changing it. The conundrum of leadership is this: people want improvement, but they resist change. Our task is helping them learn to embrace change.

The vocabulary of change is very important. As we lead people to capture momentum at point A and change vehicles, we need to avoid labeling the current systems as "bad" or "ineffective," or using any other language that devalues the hard work and dedication of those who have come before us. To help people take steps into the future, we need to celebrate the past. When they feel that we truly value the past, they will be willing to let go of it and take steps forward.

In their minds (or maybe on paper), leaders need to keep a ledger during times of change. On one side of the ledger are gains, and on the other, losses. The leader casting the vision for change can list many things under gains. She sees the future, and she is convinced that the changes she proposes will propel the church to fulfill God's vision. A few other visionaries are in that column, too, but virtually everyone else, about 95 percent of the people, feels a genuine sense of loss because of the proposed change. Even small changes to a church threaten people's stability and their sense of history. Someone might grumble, "I don't want to meet in the new building because my husband and I were married in our worship center. It means the world to me." Losses always carry emotional weight.

As we stand in the pulpit or meeting room to extol the wonderful benefits of the change we are inaugurating, we feel excited about the glorious possibilities, but the vast majority of people listening to us feel only sadness. No wonder they are resistant. If we don't connect with their hearts and win them, they start to question our motives and our wisdom to lead them. To bring them along, we have to recognize their losses, celebrate the past, grieve with them, and lead them gently into the future. If we don't take these compassionate steps, we effectively communicate that we don't care about their feelings or their history. In our communication about change, we want them to be convinced, "He understands what's meaningful to me. He wants to move us forward, but he celebrates the past. I can follow a leader like that."

All change is a critique of the past, and we need to be sensitive and wise as we talk about the past our people treasure.

QUO VADIS

Now, at the end of the book, which way will you go? This is not the kind of book that you breeze through, picking up a principle or two and moving on to something else. Either you embrace the process of transforming a culture and devote yourself to the hard but rewarding work, or you put the book down and go back to business as usual. There's not much middle ground. Those who take up the challenge are in for the ride of their lives. Very few tasks are as stimulating and difficult, but seeing a culture change in front of our eyes is a glorious thing to behold. The early stage is often the most difficult. Misunderstandings and resistance threaten to stop us in our tracks, but if we have the courage to keep moving forward, people begin to get it, and they become allies. Changing the culture of a team or a church forces us to delve below the surface and confront our motives and our systems. It's not for the fainthearted, but it's worth it. I hope you're in—all in.

NOTES

1. Dick Clark quoted in "Corporate Culture Is the Game,"

2. Patrick Lencioni, *The Five Dysfunctions of a Team* (San Francisco: Jossey-Bass, 2002), pp. 188–189.

3. Dave Logan, John King, and Halee Fisher-Wright, "Corporate Tribes: The Heart of Effective Leadership," *Leader to Leader*, Summer 2008, pp. 25–29.